ROBIN LAING is a songwriter and occasional poet with a particular passion for good whisky, which he thinks might be Scotland's greatest contribution to humanity.

He frequently performs his whisky songs, poems and stories at whisky festivals, whisky dinners, Burns Suppers and many other events (usually involving a wee taste of the subject matter of course).

Robin also writes tasting notes for the Scotch Malt Whisky Society and, having been immersed in whisky (not literally!) for decades, he now knows a thing or two about its history and its production.

Originally from Edinburgh, he now lives in rural South Lanarkshire, touring extensively both in the UK and overseas. He has recorded nine CDs, five of which contain only whisky songs – *The Angels' Share*, *The Water of Life*, *One for the Road*, *Whisky for Breakfast* and *Whisky and Death*. He is the author of three other Luath publications – *The Whisky Muse*, *The Whisky River* and *Whisky Legends of Islay*.

BOB DEWAR was born at an early age in Edinburgh.
First published at 14, and in print every day since.
Political and social commentary for *The Scotsman*.
12 books for Oxford University Press.
Illustrates for The Scotch Malt Whisky Society, Leith.
Married to author Isla Dewar.
Two sons. Two Siamese cats.
No mention in the *Senchus Fer nAlban*.

I

The Whisky Muse II

More Poems and Songs Inspired by
Scotland's National Drink

ROBIN LAING

Illustrated by
Bob Dewar

Luath Press Limited
EDINBURGH
www.luath.co.uk

First Published 2018

Reprinted 2021

ISBN: 978-1-912147-60-1

CONTENTS

Introduction 9

Poems 11

I   INSPIRING BOLD JOHN BARLEYCORN

    In Praise of Barley   14
    Cooperage Reflections   15
    Ode to Peat   16
    A Bonded Warehouse is a Magic Place   17
    Tasting Note 1 : Kissing a Balrog's Bum   19
    Tasting Note 2 : Sea-shells on a Sandy Shore   20
    The Whisky Collector   21

II   IT'S WHISKY TIME

    Darkest Secrets   24
    Hibernation   25
    Written on the Ferry to Islay, St Andrew's Day   27
    Whisky in the Snow   30
    A Whisky Kiss   31
    Viagra Whisky   33

III   THE SPIRIT OF THE PLACE

    Ardbeg   36
    Bowmore Miscellany   37
    The Sea Dragon   40
    The Maid of Islay   44
    Smokey the Cat   48
    Miscellaneous Whisky Limericks   50
    The Rabbit Wars of Cardrona   52

IV   WHISKY AND FOOD

    The Truth about Haggis   56
    Bowmore Oysters   59
    A'bunadh and Chocolate   61
    Address to the Whisky Baba   63
    Two Triolets for Martine Nouet   65
    Ideas for a Scotch Whisky Dinner   66

Songs

V	**THE BEST DRINK IN THE WORLD**	
	More Than Just a Dram	74
	The Barley Bree	76
	Whisky for Breakfast	77
	Whisky and Death	80
	Special Sipping Whisky	82
	Slow as Molasses	84
	World of Whisky	86
	The Wintertime is Coming	88
VI	**THESE ARE A FEW OF MY FAVOURITE DRAMS**	
	Talisker Bay	90
	Macallan	92
	A'bunadh	94
	The Arran Dram	96
	A Turquoise Frame of Mind	98
	The Bruichladdich Dram	100
	Black Art	102
VII	**WHISKY HEROES**	
	All the Whisky Men	106
	Old Minmore	109
	Elijah Craig	111
	Paul Campbell	113
	Magic Ship of Dreams	115
	The Boys at Bruichladdich	117
	Pestering Jim	119
VIII	**RELATIONSHIPS**	
	Monkey Shoulder	122
	Heaven Hill	124
	Johnnie and Me	126
	The Wee Cooper o' Fife	129
	Ugly Betty	132
	Whisky Widow	135

IX	WHISKY IN ITS PLACE	
	The Speyside Whisky Song	138
	Reaching Home	140
	Bruichladdich	142
	Whisky Cathedral	144
	Islay Roads	146
	The Hills of Ardnahoe	148
	Jasper 'Jack' D.	149
	The Smallest Whisky Bar	151
	The *Sentosa* Sails Away	153
X	NOTHING SUCCEEDS LIKE EXCESS	
	Oh Lord	156
	Usquebaugh Baul	158
	We can't let Al Qaeda get their Hands on This	160
	Loons is Loons	162
	Shackleton's Hut	164
	The Missionary	166
	Snuffed Out	169

Introduction

My first whisky book was *The Whisky Muse* – subtitled 'Scotch Whisky in Poem and Song' – published in 2002. At that time I was getting excited about collecting songs and poems on the theme of whisky, performing them and making CD recordings. Over the years I seem somehow to have drifted or shifted from collecting material to writing and composing it. It remains true that whisky is a subject I am passionate about and there is still enormous scope for more poems, more stories, more musings, more songs – and more drinking enjoyment. I also spend some of my time and creativity writing tasting notes for the Scotch Malt Whisky Society. I'm just one of those lucky people who find inspiration as well as pleasure in a glass of good single malt.

However, I reached the age where most people retire and although I did not have a huge desire to give up drinking whisky and singing for a living, I did at least get an urge to tidy up, to create order and to draw some kind of line under the stuff I have produced in twenty or so years of having Scotch whisky as my muse. So I present here an oeuvre of my whisky-inspired work to date. I do write about other subjects too, but whisky is not just a thread in my writing; it's a tapestry in its own right – a Bayeux-style embroidered tableau depicting the conquest of whisky over my rational, sensible self. It is not possible that the reader could have as much fun reading this stuff as I had in producing it – but I hope it will give some entertainment.

The illustrations have been created by Bob Dewar (as with my other whisky books) and it looks like he had fun too. I first met artistic genius Bob when he was illustrating for the Scotch Malt Whisky Society; his illustrations still grace the ceiling of the Members' Room at the Vaults in Leith, like some Sistine Chapel representation of a well-known story, only instead of God and Adam, the centrepiece could be the barman handing a glass of heavenly nectar to the thirsty customer.

I have split the book into two main sections – poems and songs. I am primarily a songwriter, though I try my hand at (mostly light) verse too. Songs are harder as you have to compose a tune as well as the words, but then with poems the words are somehow more naked and exposed (and some of the poetic forms impose fiendish structural disciplines), so for me they are different enough enterprises that I wanted to present them that way. Within each section I have found sub-themes, for no particular reason other than that's the way my mind works. I have decided not to include the music for the songs, though each song has a reference to where the tune might be found. In addition, if anyone would like help with the guitar chords I would be happy to respond to e-mails.

I hope these songs and poems might appeal to whisky drinkers and non-whisky drinkers – even non-drinkers – alike. Uisge-beatha is so much part of Scotland's culture, history and identity that it deserves a wider interest and attention than just the eager salivations of the whisky imbiber. And after all, stories are still stories. But if you do take an occasional dram you might find that enjoyment of these ramblings and ruminations is enhanced by a glass of the amber nectar.

Slainte Mhath

Robin Laing
www.robinlaing.com

Poems

Oh whisky! soul o' plays and pranks!
Accept a Bardie's gratefu' thanks!
When wanting thee, what tuneless cranks
  Are my poor verses!
Thou comes — they rattle i' their ranks,
  At ither's arses.

ROBERT BURNS; 'SCOTCH DRINK'

Inspiring Bold John Barleycorn

Poems inspired by the craft and character of 'the cratur'.

In Praise of Barley
Cooperage Reflections
Ode to Peat
A Bonded Warehouse is a Magic Place
Tasting Note 1: Kissing a Balrog's Bum
Tasting Note 2: Sea-shells on a Sandy Shore
The Whisky Collector

In Praise of Barley

POEM • VILLANELLE

I'll always sing the praise of barley grain
I'll sing it loud and from the very heart
With barley bree you'll not hear me complain

In fact I think it's whisky keeps me sane
Some love to smoke, but for my part
I'll always sing the praise of barley grain

For barley bree brings pleasure to my brain
I feel more handsome, fitter and quite smart
With barley bree you'll not hear me complain

The barley seed conjoins the sun and rain
And lends itself to our distillers' art
I'll always sing the praise of barley grain

I cannot spin a verse like La Fontaine
Or logically argue like Descartes
With barley bree you'll not hear me complain

Although I have my share of aches and pains
And maybe someday soon will fall apart
I'll always sing the praise of barley grain
With barley bree you'll not hear me complain

I am not the first to sing the praise of barley. Robert Burns did it much more eloquently. Scotland does not have the climate to grow vines — but barley makes such a wonderful alternative. Of all the things that spirits can be made from, there is no doubt in my mind that malted barley creates the best drink, by far.

Cooperage Reflections

POEMS • HAIKU

From barley to drams
From acorn to oak to cask
It all starts with seeds

A hundred summers
Drizzled honey on this tree
Now it sweetens drams

Mighty oaks are felled;
Their death gifts colour and taste
To *uisge beatha*

> *I wrote the script for the Speyside Cooperage's visitor centre video. While working on it I couldn't resist throwing in a few haiku.*

Ode to Peat

POEM • SONNET

Wee rough and crumbly, fibrous cake o' peat
I love your perfumed smoke, I love your heat.
In summertime we cut you from the bog
In wintertime we burn you like a log.
Your heady haze adorns each village street;
All island people love the reek o' peat.
And what would all the whisky makers do
If they couldn't pinch a bit of smoke from you?
Without a tiny thread or wisp of smoke
All whisky drinkers cough and retch and choke.
For real men need the rasping edgy stuff
And Islay women like a bit of rough!
A smoky flavoured dram cannot be beat
So here's to you - you handsome slab o' peat!

Malt whisky has only three simple ingredients — water, malted barley and yeast, but there are other things that can influence the taste very significantly — especially the wood it is matured in and the amount of peat used in the process of drying the barley. For some people, peated whiskies, especially the Islay ones, are the most desirable.

A Bonded Warehouse is a Magic Place

POEM • VILLANELLE

A bonded warehouse is a magic place
With hogsheads, butts and barrels, row on row
To spend a day inside one would be ace

In fact I'd like to have one as a base
Poetic inspiration there would flow
A bonded warehouse is a magic place

I'd have to take a sleeping bag in case;
It might get cold at night in there you know
To spend a day inside one would be ace

Between the rows of barrels I would chase
Imaginary Marilyn Monroes
A bonded warehouse is a magic place

I'd be aboard a spaceship up in space
And out beyond the galaxy we'd go
To spend a day inside one would be ace

Without the pow'r of speech I'd use my face
And grimace like a mad Marcel Marceau
A bonded warehouse is a magic place
To spend a day inside one would be ace

This is just a fantasy of course, but in my opinion, the best thing that can happen on a visit to a distillery is when your host takes you into the warehouse and pops the bungs on one or two casks, dips the valinch and splashes a dram, straight from the cask into your glass. A magical experience, the real McCoy, original sin, forbidden fruit, child in a sweetie shop – all rolled into one moment!

Kissing a Balrog's Bum

POEM • TASTING NOTE FOR A 1989 SINGLE CASK LAPHROAIG

Our noses were dazzled and bacon-frazzled
By seaweed (cut and dried),
Coal in a casket, a new-made basket
With orange and bread inside;
A doctor's bag; a fire-cooked prawn
And grilled black pudding (with sugar on!).
'Oh wow! What a nose' we cried.

The taste was fierce with embers and ash
Hawaiian pork, cooked in a pit;
Our tongues were roasted, twisted and lashed
By the peppery, liquorice hit.
A honey sweet, marshmallow treat
And egg custard were pleasing to some,
But someone said 'Ooooh! Incinerated shoe';
While another kissed a Balrog's bum *
And ran, whimpering, home to his mum.

* Balrog – a fiery demon from *The Lord of the Rings*

If I remember correctly, this was a smoky whisky from a sherry cask — that is a combination that does not have universal appeal. Not everyone loves sherry matured drams and not everyone loves smoky whiskies. The comments from the tasting panel at the Scotch Malt Whisky Society were therefore quite mixed — but after adding up the scores, the whisky had passed and I felt the need to express not only the positive comments.

Sea-shells on a Sandy Shore

POEM • TASTING NOTE FOR A 1991 CAOL ILA

Nose

Aberdeen harbour – Arbroath smokie
Dolly Mixtures, leather, oaky
Gorse and brambles, soap and soot
Mineral, meadows, tar and fruit
Stretchy bandage, and what's more
Sea-shells on a sandy shore
Germolene and a Barbour jacket
Lime on slate – ye canna whack it

Palate

The likes o' this ye've never tastit
Savour each drop – dinnae waste it
It's nice an fruity for a start
Currants, lemons, rhubarb tart
A tin of travel sweets is pleasing
Gentle smoke is lightly teasing
The ash is there – dinna quarrel
Then juicy bubble-gum and sorrel
A dram for any time or place
To bring a smile to every face

Sometimes the notes scribbled down while tasting a whisky just seem to lend themselves to a story or a poem. It is quite common for the aromas from a smoky island whisky to evoke impressions or memories of a maritime nature.

The Whisky Collector

POEM

The whisky collector is a very sad guy
His impulse is not to drink but to buy
He would not understand a guy such as I
My way of seeing, my way of thinking
That whisky is not to keep, but for drinking

The whisky collector wakes up each day
And admires his bottles out on display
He counts and caresses, then puts them away
Takes joy just from looking, touching and clinking
He never gives into the pleasure of drinking

He keeps his neat stash in a shed or a den
Alphabetically ordered – his Bens and his Glens
He counts all his bottles again and again
To be sure his collection is growing, not shrinking
But how could it shrink, when it isn't for drinking?

The whisky collector is usually male
His fun mostly comes at the point of a sale
Each bottle he owns has a story or tale
Which he tells with his wee beady eye never blinking
His passion is real – but never for drinking!

At the end of the day, when we go to the pub
Backs to slap and shoulders to rub
The whisky collector shovels his grub
But when it's his round, to the door he is slinking
For he doesn't quite get this mad social drinking

The whisky collector is naught but a pest
When sanely considered and put to the test
His only mantra is 'buy and invest'
He's never heard of 'responsible drinking'
(Which means don't buy whisky you don't intend sinking)

When a whisky collector finally croaks
There's a lump in my throat, that near makes me choke
For his children will drink his best stuff – mixed with Coke
May he meet the same fate as Araham Lincoln
'Twould serve him right – for collecting, not drinking!

> I like to have a go at whisky collectors – saying that whisky is surely made to be drunk, not kept under lock and key – but maybe the truth is that I am just jealous because I can't afford the price of rare whiskies these days.

II

It's Whisky Time!

'When is the right time to drink this Black Art whisky?'
someone asked Jim McEwan at an event in Germany
— 'What time do you get up in the morning?' he replied.

Darkest Secrets
Hibernation
Written on the Ferry to Islay, St Andrew's Day
Whisky in the Snow
A Whisky Kiss
Viagra Whisky

Darkest Secrets

POEM • SONNET

Real magic happens on the darkest nights,
When shades and shadows conspire to confuse;
The half-heard whisper tingles and excites;
The fleeting brush of hair, the scuff of shoes.
There may be dangers — there may be delights;
Will you accept your fate and not accuse?
The teeth of possibility might bite
The toes of those with little left to lose.

Find your fortune in the wishing well,
The forest path in darkness never ends.
Night-scented blossoms have the sweetest smell,
Nocturnal creatures have the keenest sense,
And darkest secrets we should only tell
In whispers to our very dearest friends.

Bowmore Darkest is a 15 year old whisky from Islay that has been finished for three years in Oloroso sherry casks. It is one of their flagship whiskies and the gorgeous colour and heady aromas made me think of writing something teasingly enigmatic; but this poem is very much about the pleasures of the night, of which enjoying a decent, aromatic dram is surely one.

Hibernation

POEM

Now is the time to hibernate
Get to bed early – wake up late
When winter comes there's no debate
No reason to procrastinate

When worldly cares increase in weight
When rivers freeze or run in spate
And cars on icy roads will skate
This is the time of year I hate

To sleep perchance to dream – how great!
For months wrapped up in bed – first-rate
I'm simply going to incubate
Until the spring – or later date

The cold and damp debilitate
Why don't we all just emigrate?
I've tried hard to appreciate
The lack of sun – but honest mate
I really cannot contemplate
Such a fun-less, freezing fate
So here's my plan - I'm heading straight
To bed – right now – tonight at eight
I know it will infuriate
My wife – she'll call me reprobate
My mind's made up – but hold on – wait!

Wake me up on Christmas Eve
Ruffle my hair and tug my sleeve
And whisper softly in my ear
Of Stollen bites and Weihnachtsbier

I'd hate to miss that Christmas morn
The piles of gifts, the tree adorned
A long lie – looking out on snow
Witrh sparkling flute of Veuve Clicquot

A lazy day while someone else
Fills the kitchen with lovely smells
Maybe a goose, maybe a duck
A big rib roast if I'm in luck

And after that some Christmas pud
A fire of scented, hissing wood
Then chocolates by the kilogram
Washed down with very special drams

And then as night-time starts to creep
I'll head for bed and back to sleep
Don't bother me on Boxing day
Just let me sleep till Hogmanay

The older I get, the more wearisome I find the Scottish winters and I often fantasise about emigration and hibernation; but then I remember the crisp days walking in the snowy hills, the fun, frolics and feasting of Christmas and Hogmanay, the log fire, candles and drams of winter hygge – and I somehow manage to cope. From late Autumn, when the trees start to take on the hue of matured whisky, through to the first warm kiss of spring, whisky helps those of us who live in Northern climes to stay positive and avoid the gloom.

Written on the Ferry to Islay, St Andrew's Day

POEM • STANDARD HABBIE

In Bowmore toon there staun's a wunder
That whusky freaks wid like tae plunder
It's been aroon' since seventeen hunder
An' seventy nine
An' shows nae sign o' slippin under
The wheels o' time

Within its warehoose casks are sleepin'
Secure within the angels' keepin'
While time an' tide are slowly creepin'
Inch by inch
How happy Ah wid be tae sneak in
Wi' a valinch

St Andrew, patron o' this Nation
Save us fi intoxication
We'll be content wi' moderation
Nae hardcore
There's nae harm in a wee sensation
O' guid Bowmore

Whenever we are feelin' peeky
Hirplin', stiff, crank an' creaky
We don't want nae cockaleekie
Or Cullen Skink
What will mak' us cheerie, cheeky?
Oor national drink!

If only Ah wis rich an' famous
Like Calvin Klein or Nostradamus
Ah'd sit a' day in silk pyjamas
You can be sure
Sniffin', sippin', sookin' drammies
O' auld Bowmore

A daily dose o' Scotch an' soda
Can mak' ye wise like Master Yoda
Hoots mon, that is jist a load a
Star Wars guff
But underneath Bowmore's pagodas
There's astral stuff

Distillery cats are weel-kent moggies
Celebretised oan whisky bloggies
In olden days the boys wore doggies
Strapped tae ther legs
Tae pinch an inch fi butts an' hoggies
Or ither kegs

Dear Saint, we praise yer banes an' relics
Apostolic, evangelic
Wi' just a touch o' whisky medic
(It's jist the biz!)
Yer creed wad be mair psychedelic
Than it is

St Andrew! Spiritual protector
There's nae need for wild conjecture
If ye want the res perfecta
That we adore
Jist tak a gless o' amber nectar
An auld Bowmore

It is a shame that here in Scotland we don't make more of our national Saint and celebrate his day the way the Irish do with St Patrick. Maybe it is because we are too dour and Protestant!

Whisky in the Snow

POEM • VILLANELLE

The glass you now hold in your hand is cold
But it contains a liquid sunset fire
And heart and soul are warmed by glow of gold

All day we watched a snowy scene unfold
Banks and drifts of snow grew ever higher
The glass you now hold in your hand is cold

Now here we stand and precious drops we hold
What better contrast could a man desire
As heart and soul are warmed by glow of gold?

In whisky, tales of summertime are told
Ripe barley and the happy songbirds' choir
The glass you now hold in your hand is cold

The snow is fresh and new; the whisky old
The land has donned a linen white attire
As heart and soul are warmed by glow of gold

We sip and find our spirits are made bold
And more and more we can the scene admire
The glass you now hold in your hand is cold
But heart and soul are warmed by glow of gold

There is something about enjoying a dram on a winter's evening in front of a roaring fire that is hard to beat, but as someone who enjoys walking in the Scottish hills in all seasons of the year, I have to say that the finest pleasure of all is taking a warming dram with friends on the summit of some snow-covered peak as a reward for having made it to the top, or at the end of the walk — or sometimes both! This poem tries to capture the contrast, the yin and yang, of the cold, white, new snow and the warm, old, golden spirit.

A Whisky Kiss

POEM

Down in the deep, dark heat
of the pot still, bound by copper plate,
our love was forged.

It started out with just a sip
but even then we knew
that somewhere else –
in rivet's grip,
a force-fed pressure,
pushing upwards, seeking space,
would determine that our essences
should mingle, merge,
combine and interlace.

Unimaginable energy at play,
seething, surging, bursting at the boil.
the cauldron of a witch;
the quest of alchemist;
the blow-out after drilling oil;
the surface of a sun a trillion miles away.

And from that first intensity
this special spirit flowed,
fed by fire and smoke;
a liquid love encased
in harvested and crafted wood;
tempered strength inside a stronger oak
to hold it in for decades, firm and fast.

'Nectar and ambrosia distilled'
the fateful words the Cyclops spoke,
(before his frightful arrogance was felled),
and that was only wine – but this!
The promise of a never-ending wish,
a pleasure first to last,
a loving, breathing, bonding whisky kiss.

The process of making whisky somehow reflects the diurnal rhythm of our human existence – the milling, mashing, fermentation and distillation stages are full of energy and activity – then the maturation is quiet, sleeping, down time – a wonderful balance. Come to think of it, that pattern – energy followed by peacefulness – also reflects the progress of many a successful love relationship; and by the way, the best time to drink expensive whisky is when you are in love.

Viagra Whisky

POEM • VILLANELLE

Viagra whisky is a good idea
I've done the research and I know it's true
Although the price can make you shed a tear

Do not use blended whisky though; for fear
'Distiller's dangle' leaves you in a stew
The best malt whisky is a good idea –

From sherry casks and over fifteen years
Is what you must use when you wish to woo
(Although the price can make you shed a tear)

This balladeer is really quite sincere
But please do not my warning misconstrue
Viagra whisky is a good idea

But it can make your legs and arms feel queer –
A total loss of feeling that you'll rue
And so the price can make you shed a tear

Despite the loss of feeling, persevere
A jelly-fish waving a stick will do!
Viagra whisky is a good idea
Although the price can make you shed a tear

Maybe it's the rhythmic passion of the Flamenco dancers – or something to do with the Spanish Fly – but cask strength, sherry cask matured single malt of reasonable age has interesting effects on one's romantic feelings and libido. Aberlour A'bunadh does the job just fine; or Glendronach 18; or a nice old Glenfarclas; or any decent sherry-wood dram from the SMWS – but do watch out for the side effects!

III

The Spirit of the Place

Whisky can have a connection with the place where it was made,
or even the place where it was drunk.

Ardbeg
Bowmore Miscellany
The Sea Dragon
The Maid of Islay
Smokey the Cat
Miscellaneous Whisky Limericks
The Rabbit Wars of Cardrona

Ardbeg

POEM

I saw shafts of sun –
heard the flutter of wings;
a rainbow kissed dappled water.

The malt barn held only ladders
and history played in the shadows
but new wood and fresh mortar
held the promise that sings –
'The still runs again in Ardbeg!'

After long years of sleep behind briers,
colour returns and the heat
bubbles and re-energizes;
the phoenix finally rises
from ashes of peat
and pirouettes on a fine leg.

I visited Ardbeg distillery shortly after it reopened in 1997 after being purchased by Glenmorangie. I always feel sad when good distilleries are mothballed – and then happy when they are re-opened. Ardbeg was such an iconic distillery and brand that this seemed to warrant a poem.

Bowmore Miscellany

POEM • LIMERICKS

There was a young man from Bowmore
Who decided to go on a splore
When he woke up next day
He'd spent all his pay
And what's more – his body was sore.

An elderly man in Bowmore
Discovered his son's whisky store
He waded right in
And declared with a grin
'This is better than *Whisky Galore!*'

A hero who came from Bowmore
Single-handedly stopped the Cold War
He showed all the Russkies
Our fabulous whuskies
And established a peaceful rapport.

Warehouse One at Bowmore
Once decided to open its door
When the folk got inside
One of them cried
'I'm a child in a big candy store!'

When Hamlet came to Bowmore
He was homesick for old Elsinore
But Eddie said 'Hammie,
Jist hae a wee drammie
And dinna be such an auld bore'.

Some say that the scent of Bowmore
Has more than a touch of French whore
Just show them to me
They'll be over my knee
Imploring 'No more, zut alors!'

In the central square of Bowmore
Is a sculpture by bold Henry Moore
It's made out of brass
It's a bottle and glass
In a frieze of perpetual pour

A maltman who came from Bowmore
To his wife and his children once swore
That he'd never drink more
Than just three or four
But he lied and had more than a score.

To drink a wee dram o' Bowmore
Is hardly a difficult chore
I would rather do that
Than clean up my flat
For that is a thing I abhor.

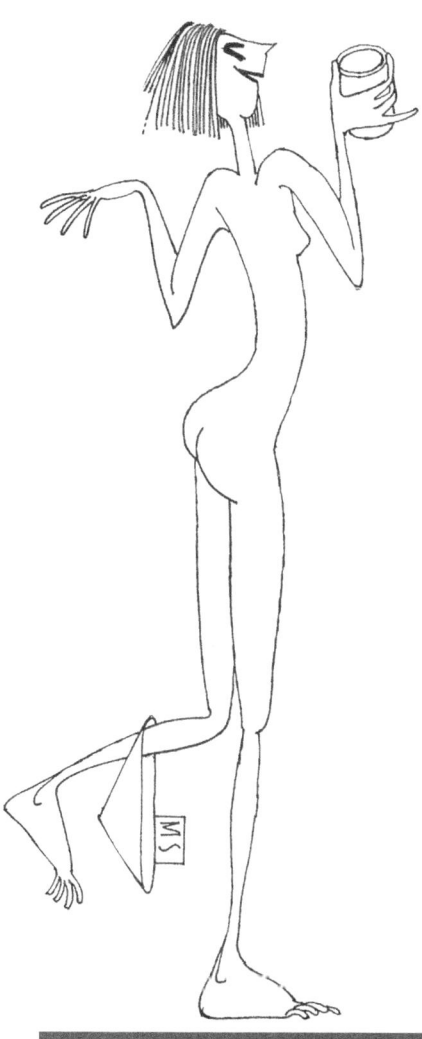

An Indian came to Bowmore
And said, 'What is this whisky for?'
They gave him a taste
He was simply amazed
And declared it was true Koh-I-Noor.

I once had a shy paramour
So I gave her a dram of Bowmore
She finished her drink
With a smile and a wink
Then dropped all her clothes to the floor.

In Bowmore where the white birds soar
And the sun shines down on the shore
You can stand on the sand
With a dram in your hand
And your spirits will be restored.

I know a man – Eddie MacAffer
At Bowmore he is now the gaffer
He plies me with drink
And says 'What do you think?'
Then mocks me with cynical laughter.

A lady by name Rachel Barrie
Is someone I'm anxious to marry
I think in the end
We'd make a fine blend
And I'd be as happy as Larry.

Once I get going with Limericks I find it hard to stop – a bit like drinking good Bowmore! I've long had an admiration for Bowmore, right back to the days when Jim McEwan was the manager, but Eddie MacAffer was the distillery manager and Rachel Barrie was the master blender at the time when I wrote these.

The Sea Dragon

POEM

From Bowmore shore he rowed his boat
Out on Lochindaal
Rainbow drops from dripping oar
The rhythmic rise and fall

The sun shone strong, the sky full blue
The water smooth and calm
His boat was light and seemed to float
Like a feather on a palm

He rowed her round beyond Gartbreck
And turned her, steering south
Past Laggan Point and on into
The island's gaping mouth

He shipped the oars to give his limbs
A welcome pause and rest;
He slept upon the ocean's softly,
Gently rising breast

Then with a flash, a crack, a crash
His dreamy peace was snapped
The boat spun round like a waltzter;
Thunder roared and clapped

A storm was raging all around
More than just a squall
Tossed on the black and angry deep
He felt so lone and small

So dark the sky – there was no trace
Or hint of land in sight
Through rain and spray he strained his eyes
Searching for a light

The sea was breaking all around
White horses leaping high
The din more frightening to his ears
Than heathen battle cry

He feared the storm, he blamed himself
Humbled by the gale
He shivered at the prospect that
His battered boat might fail

Beneath him rising through the sea
He heard an eerie sound
An evil, grating, shriek; the roar
Of monstrous beast unbound

A boiling surge around him broke
Great turmoil in the sea
He racked his brains and bit his hand
What could this danger be?

Then childhood tales came to his mind
Of Fingal and his hounds
And fell sea-dragons that appear
The moment someone drowns

At other times he would have said
Such things could not be true
But now he knew this violent sea
Was bringing Kranna Dubh

He swept the hair out of his eyes
And grabbed the jerking oars
His only thought to flee – before
The great sea dragon roars

He pulled and pulled with all his strength
He didn't care which way
He knew he had to reach some shore
To live another day

All his skin was taut with fear
His back bent like a bow
Praying fate would keep him from
The cliffs around the Oa

It seemed an age but finally
His boat scraped up on sand
And gratefully he threw himself
Upon the Laggan Strand

He made his way on foot to town
Through darkness, wind and rain
And many moons would come and go
Before he'd row again

The weary lad reached home at last
His body stiff and sore
The medicine he needed most –
Thirty-year-old Bowmore

Another Islay legend — and another tale once used on a Bowmore bottling. I have tasted the thirty year old Sea Dragon expression from Bowmore — a delightful dram, but hard to get these days — it is becoming almost legendary itself.

The Maid of Islay

POEM

In days of yore, a few years before
The distillery came to Bowmore
A church quite round was built in the town
And the local folks' morals did soar

They built the church round, so no spot could be found
Where the Devil could sneak in and hide
They feared Old Nick, but were up to his tricks
So they left not a corner inside

But arrogant Satan believed his temptations
Weak mortals could never refuse
So he came to Bowmore and sneaked in the door
With offers of sex, drugs and booze

The dour congregation, not seduced by temptation
Proceeded to chase him around
Wi' no corner to hide in, he wasnae for bidin'
So he fled from the church like a hound

Down Bowmore main street on his big cloven feet
He ran with his tail in his hand
Pursued by that crowd, indignant and proud
Was more than Auld Hornie could stand

At the foot of the hill, where the Bowmore distil-
ery stood near the harbour wall
The Devil slipped in, between the malt bins
And they just couldn't find him at all

For hours they looked, every cranny and nook
Above and below and behind
Inside the malt mill and under each still
Not a trace of Mahoun could they find

Long after the knell of the midnight bell
They gave up and slouched off to their beds
But they left the door barred and they posted a guard
Someone trusty who'd not be misled

About two in the morning a whistle gave warning
That a boat was about to set sail
T'was only the *Maid of Islay*, whose trade
Was in whisky, the Gael's holy grail

She slid from her mooring, her cargo secure
Her paddles pounding the foam
From harbour wall, into dark Lochindaal
Heading for Glasgow and home

It soon became clear that the Devil, through fear
Of the Presbyterian horde
Had slipped like an eel himself to conceal
In a cask and got loaded on board

We can only suppose (nobody knows,
For the *Maid* was never more seen)
That the fate of her crew, six good men and true
Was something grotesque and obscene

As the years slip away from that terrible day
The memory fades in our heads
But still now and then, distillery men
Hear noises that fill them with dread

It could just be the wind, with waves combined
Hitting the warehouse wall
But the man in the street would swear t'was the beat
Of paddles on Lochindaal

Some local folk claim that now and again
The Devil comes close to the shore
For over the years, his taste, it appears
Has turned to a dram of Bowmore

But he relives the fear from the time he was here
Chased by angels and big bearded men
For he cursed then and swore that Hell would freeze o'er
Ere he'd come back to Islay again

So he gnashes his teeth, in anger and grief
Unable to get new supplies
And now you can see why Islay is free
From wickedness, mischief and lies

> *It is a great story — the legend of the* Maid *of Islay. All I have done here is to turn it into a poem — and add the wee touches of imagining the Devil having a craving for the whisky. This version of the tale explains why you never feel the need to lock your door while on Islay.*

Smokey the Cat

POEM

Smokey the cat came from nowhere;
Just whisped in under some door;
Sniffed quietly around
And knew that she'd found
The best place to stay in Bowmore.

She'd arrived at Bowmore distillery
Where the finest malt whisky is made.
There was no welcome mat
For Smokey the cat
But she liked the place – so she stayed.

They say cats have more than one life
With re-incarnation and that.
Whether it's true
All that cat deja vu,
Smokey's a born again cat.

There's something about her that takes you
Back to the Lords of the Isles
When the cats of Finlaggan
Would go scallywaggin'
For miles and miles and miles.

It's the way she melts into the shadows
Or suddenly creeps up on folk
She'll always find you
Slinking behind you
The cat who was named after smoke.

She sits on the sill of the maltings
On days when the weather is nice
And while one eye sleeps
The other one keeps
A lookout for small birds and mice.

Small birds and mice eat the barley
So Smokey confronts them foursquare
But she pulls in her claws
And quietly ignores
The Angels who come for their share.

Felines don't care for whisky
Everyone understands that
But that peaty odour
Beneath the pagoda
Owes something to Smokey the cat.

On Islay people made whisky
Long before it was chic;
The cat from Bowmore
Is nothing more
Than the ghost of the island's peat-reek.

The first time I visited Bowmore distillery I was introduced to Smokey, the distillery cat. She is no longer around but her memory lives on in this.

Miscellaneous Whisky Limericks

POEM • LIMERICKS

She was sad in the Schwann in Horgen
Her only intent – to explore gin
But Hedwig poured whisky
Which made her quite frisky
A lesson she's gladly absorbin'.

I rely on my friends Brad and Ina
To provide me with drams that are finer
I don't give a damn
For other folks' drams
The Society's drams are diviner.

The Scotch Malt Whisky Society
Is a place where you don't find much piety
No vain huff and puff
Or political guff
And certainly not much sobriety.

A lassie that came from Lochmaben
Spent a whisky weekend in a cabin
With a guy in a kilt
Who was massively built
And whom she was constantly grabbin'.

There was a young man from Lauffen
Who too much whisky was kaufen
Until one sad day
He spent all his pay
On a 40 year old that was bowfin'.

A man from Lauffen am Neckar
Pronounced 'this whisky is lecker'
But then he got drunk
As drunk as a skunk
And lost the use of his pecker.

The Angels' Share man Peter Hofmann
Invented a malt lover's coffin
There's a link to ground level
By a tube to a barrel
Now the locals are dying too often.

There was a young lady from Gore
Who drank some whisky liqueur
The Old Hokonui
Went Wham! and Kablooie!
And she ended up on the floor.

The Limerick is a simple but versatile poetic form; you can compose them quite easily and leave a scattering of little records of your having passed through — like Robert Burns composing lines on windows, napkins and menus — or like a dog that takes care to water every other tree along the avenue of life.

So, as I travel around doing whisky events all over the place, I often amuse myself by scribbling Limericks about the places or the people. Mostly, they are ephemeral and contribute nothing to posterity; these are just a few that I found in my notebook. Brad and Ina run the Scotch Malt Whisky Society in Switzerland and in nearby Oberentfelden Peter Hofmann, whisky writer and enthusiast, has the whisky shop and restaurant called The Angels' Share. The Phoenix (in Lauffen am Neckar, Germany) is an Irish pub with an impressive selection of Scotch single malts, and Gore is in South Island, New Zealand, where I performed at the Hokonui Moonshine Museum.

The Rabbit Wars of Cardrona

POEM

The pesky wabbits of Wanaka
Came up the Crown Range Road
They dug themselves in at Cardrona
Right next to the Curtis abode

They were tired of living in Wanaka
And an exodus seemed the best plan
For hundreds of them had been
    flattened
By a succession of fast campervans

But Cardrona seemed almost perfect
With pasture, tree, bush and hedge
With soil that was easy to burrow
Not to mention the Curtis's veg

But springtime came round to
    Cardrona
And activities filled the air
Folk Festival time was approaching
And they didn't want wabbitses there

For rabbits in springtime do frolic
And openly fornicate too
For the ladies and blokies
Who call themselves folkies
Such wantonness just wouldn't do

For them, breeding and procreation
Are buried long in the past
And they don't need reminded
They'd rather stay blinded
To all the joys that they've lost

So Martin got up one fine morning
Grabbed his gun, put his hunting cap
    on
He swore he'd make war on the warren
And not rest till the rabbits were gone

With metres and metres of rabbit wire
He put fences around the whole site
With quite a bit buried beneath the
    ground
To make the security tight

He went out with his gun and took
    pot-shots —
Any rabbit that popped up its head
Before they could scatter for cover
A score or more lay there dead

Then he blocked up their holes with
    boulders
And set up a few cunning traps
He even set loose a Chihuahua
That scared them with barking and yaps

He poured boiling water down some
    holes
With a glint in his eye and a shout
And thought it tremendously funny
When a hot cross bunny jumped out

And so he retired that first day
Convinced that the battle was won
Singing a snatch of a song from the
    past
That went 'Run rabbit — run, run, run'

But during the night at the campsite
Something curious came to pass
The late night revelling campers
Had left out some Scotch in a glass

A single malt from Islay
Bunnahabhain was what it was called
And when the bunnies were havin'
The neat Bunnahabhain
The effect was like Asterix the Gaul

The magic potion gave strength
Super powers, courage and more
With the neat Bunnahabhain
They were in Bunny Heaven
And Lords of Cardrona once more

They hared down the hill in their
    hundreds
And bared their front teeth for a fight
They gnawed through the fence
And their claws ripped the tents
And a terrible row split the night

For one was Jack Rabbit the Ripper
And another was Hop-timus Prime
The whisky had made them all frisky as
    hell
And they would repay Martin's crime

But the number one Chief of the
    Warren
Big as a Canadian moose
Was Scottish by blood
From whiskers to fud
And they called him Rabbit the Bruce

The Bruce stood tall in the middle
And passed the order around
They were thumping their feet
To a synchronised beat
That shook the Cardrona campground

The folkies all fled in a panic
There was nothing more to discuss
They thought that some bodhran
    players
Had arrived in the night by bus

So the rabbits now reign supreme
Among eucalyptus and spruce
And Martin and Kay
Both rue the day
That they tangled with Rabbit the Bruce

On my second tour of New Zealand in 2017, I was a guest at Martin Curtis's Folk Festival in Cardrona, near the popular tourist town of Wanaka in South Island. When I arrived at Cardrona preparations were underway – including various attempts to deter or destroy an invasive population of rabbits. Bush poetry performance is a regular part of the programme at the Cardrona Folk Festival, so I sat in the sunshine, with a nice cup of tea and wrote this.

It seemed to go down well and over the course of the weekend a respectable number of drams were consumed by Martin, myself and some other friends (including a Bhutanese 'Blended Scotch Whisky' called K5 – that was a first for me). I had a further chance to perform the poem when I did a whisky tasting and concert in the excellent Pembroke Wines & Spirits in Wanaka.

IV

Whisky and Food

Haggis, oysters, chocolate, cheese – whisky goes with anything (or nothing).

The Truth about Haggis
Bowmore Oysters
A'bunadh and Chocolate
Address to the Whisky Baba
Two Triolets for Martine Nouet
Ideas for a Scotch Whisky Dinner

The Truth about Haggis

POEM • STANDARD HABBIE

To gie oor spirits a' a lift
On January twenty-fifth
We serve a dish was born o' thrift
And lack o' siller
But still it is a gourmet's gift
No jist a filler

The centre-piece o' oor Burns feast
Is celebrated west tae east
The Haggis, dear iconic beast
O' this fine nation
Deserves frae me, at vera least
An explanation.

The female beast has nice plump thighs
A slender waist and flutt'ring eyes
But aye when she the male espies
She sterts a race
And he, wi' curses, groans an' sighs
Must gie her chase

For she his am'rous hugs wad joukie
While he pursues by hook or crookie
His heart's desire – her braw bahookie
Fast disappearin'
And he, in constant want o' nookie
Collapses sweirin'

But thanks tae natural selection
His third leg's permanent erection
Has set him oan a new direction
Aroond the hill
Tae grab wi' timeous perfection
His jaunty Jill.

There follows then a brief seduction
And consummated reproduction
Then, in his blissful satisfaction
He taks a nap
And fails to take evasive action
Frae hunter's trap

For as he lies there fast asleep
Smilin' – smug, on hillside steep
The haggis hunter sneaks an' creeps
All sly and crafty
And on the hapless haggis leaps
The poor wee daftie

Haggis Hound

The haggis startles wi' alarm
And tries tae flee awa frae hairm
But though he lowps an' twists an'
   squirms
Wi' dust and din
Wi's third leg in its present form
He canna rin!

Now when you through the windae look
In butcher's shop, on butcher's hook
Ye micht hae easily mistook
A male for female
For a' commercial gobbledygook
Neglects sic detail

But female haggis, fit for roy'lty
Is tasty, juicy, fine an' salty
The male, by contrast, is but paltry
Peppery, dry
It needs a splash o' decent malt tae
Help it by.

So noo the truth ye can embrace
Twa-leggit haggises are ace
Three-leggit yins are ower base
An' no sae bonnie
But yet tae serve them's nae disgrace
When short o' money

An' should ye catch a female preg-
nant — serve it for ye should be gleg
It hings upon the highest peg
Owre ony table
That famous dish, the guid Scotch egg
Sae famed in fable

Auld men wha sup their Burns
   haggis
Enjoy the ploy o' pipes an' daggers
But softly, in amang the madness
They quietly toast
The haggis — wi' a wistfu' sadness
For whit they've lost.

I often perform at Burns Suppers, especially in Switzerland and Germany, where I take the opportunity to tease people about the haggis being a rare Scottish animal, with tufts of red hair behind its ears and three legs, one of which is short, thereby enabling it to run around the Scottish mountains where it lives. This poem is just an extension of that tease.

Bowmore Oysters

POEM

Sip the briny oyster juice
But leave the oyster in its shell;
Pour the Bowmore in a glass,
Swirl it round and have a smell;

Then sniff the oyster if you will,
You're standing on the Islay shore –
Salt and sun and iodine,
Not unlike a neat Bowmore.

Close your eyes and feel the sun
Like a woolly warming cloak;
There's lemon in the whisky now
And honey and a poke of smoke.

Pop the oyster in your mouth,
How long can you hold it in?
Pour the whisky in the shell,
Hold it steady, wipe your chin.

If you have a little mouth
Swallow down the oyster first
Followed by the Bowmore dram,
Drink it like you have a thirst;

But if your mouth is big enough,
Let the oyster swim around
In the whisky – close your eyes,
Then do the luge and swallow down.

The Bowmore and the oyster glide
Down the throat – a slippy slide
Of silky silver bathed in gold,
Both the treasures now inside.

Enjoy the after-taste a while,
The oyster whole the Bowmore neat,
Suck your gums and smack your lips,
Then pour another – and repeat.

May your life be full and joyous,
Measured in kilos not in grams:
We wish you many happy years
Coasts of oysters, casks of drams.

The first time I had oysters with Bowmore whisky on them was in the Bowmore Hotel a few years ago. I think there was more whisky on them than I realised – it was the first time I ever got drunk on oysters. The Bowmore Luge is a way of enjoying the combination of oysters and drams and if you do it correctly there are several steps – I'm not sure if I have followed them faithfully in this poem – but my way works too.

A'bunadh and Chocolate

POEMS • LIMERICKS

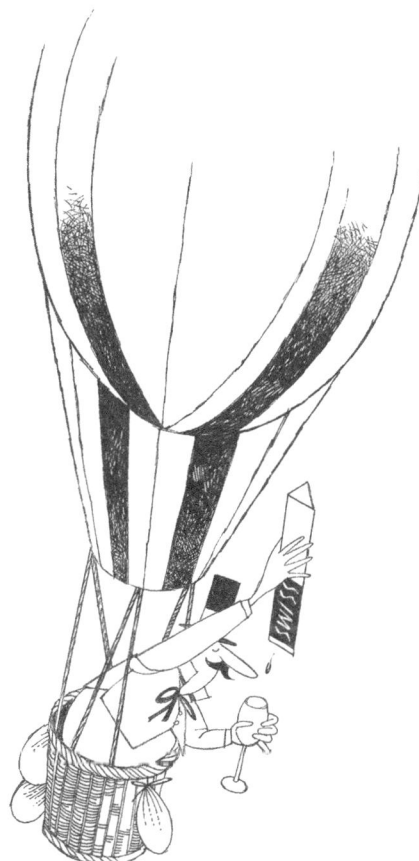

There was an old man from Corunna
Who ate chocolate dipped in A'bunadh
He said 'This great thing
Has sweetened death's sting
But I wish I'd discovered it sooner'.

There once was a hot-air ballooner
Who dined on the deck of a schooner
It ended in bliss
With dark chocolate (Swiss)
And a wine glass finned with A'bunadh.

A lady from Tristan da Cunha
Went solar and stellar and lunar
On board of a rocket
Made out of chocolate
And powered along by A'bunadh.

The German artist Maruma
Was about to be mauled by a puma
But he swiftly did act
The cat to distract
With chocolate soaked in A'bunadh.

When Carl Orff composed 'O Fortuna'
He was probably drunk on A'bunadh
But the chocolate bars
In ladies' boudoirs
Why, that's just a scandalous rumour.

That emperor, old Montezuma
Was a passionate chocolate consumer
He preferred Maya Gold
(the one Green & Blacks sold)
Always washed down with A'bunadh.

On a train between Bombay and Poona
I sat with a glass of A'bunadh
But there wasn't a drop
Of chocolate (too hot)
Which left a most empty lacuna.

In Sevilla they say that 'la luna
Es una maravilla Satsuma'
But that orange on high
Would gladden the eye
If it was chocolate laced with A'bunadh.

A ninety-year-old honeymooner
Found his bride had a poor sense of humour
When he couldn't perform
She replaced poor old Norm
With a king-size Twix and A'bunadh.

There once was a fellow named Spooner
Who fancied himself as a crooner
He sang a few bars
About bocolate chars
Which he ate with a bass of A'glunadh.

> *I whiled away an evening drinking Aberlour A'bunadh and dark chocolate and composing these ditties. Whisky and chocolate can be a winning combination — and there is something about the richness of natural strength, Oloroso matured A'bunadh which makes it a perfect partner for good chocolate. Any good chocolate will do but I like Lindt dark chocolate with sea salt and caramel or Green & Black's Maya Gold.*

Address to the Whisky Baba

POEM • STANDARD HABBIE

Fair fa' yer couthy wrinkled face
Sweet *cailleach* o' the pudding race
It canna be ta oor disgrace
If we're gaun gaga
And slaverin' at the moo to taste
The Whisky Baba!

If Scots stopped eatin' cakes an' baps
Petticoat tails an' ginger snaps
Bannocks, black bun and perhaps
A wee Baklava
The dental profession might collapse
But Whisky Baba!...

Anither gundy oan the list
And wan nae human can resist
Ignore the vile nutritionist
An' a' her patois
For noo ye can get fat AND pissed
Wi' Whisky Baba!

Now experts in domestic science
Wi' finest equipment and appliance
Even wi' insight and clairvoyance
And *tabula rasa*
Are staggered by the Auld Alliance
And its Whisky Baba!

But Martine Nouet is such a skilled yin
Her secrets she will not divulge 'em
We can but stare wi' eyeballs bulgin'
Like stoned Chihuahuas
Desperately hopin' tae indulge in
Some Whisky Baba!

A lass was singin' like a lintie
O' the meal and ale held by McGinty
Whan the pig loupt oot a first flair windae
An' doon a ladder
Just tae get its snout stuck intae
Some Whisky Baba!

Martine Nouet, author of à table: whisky from glass to plate *and an expert on combining whisky with food, was doing a whisky dinner at Aberlour distillery. She asked me if I could do a poem to go with the dessert – a whisky baba. I wrote this, modelled on the Address to the Haggis by Robert Burns. I was not able to attend the event but she got Alan Winchester, who used to be the distillery manager at Aberlour and who has a good couthy North East accent, to read it out and it apparently went down very well. Aberlour sent me two very special bottles as a reward – not bad for having a bit of fun with a few scribblings.*

When weakness has ye fash'd wi' havers
Nae energy to face your labours
Just bite the bun wi' whisky flavours
And syrup slabber'd
You'll soon be set to toss the caber
Wi' Whisky Baba!

This poet's tryin' tae mak' us wait noo
It's no quite time tae masticate you
But anither verse wid be quite hatefu'
O' blah palaver
So just tuck in tae every platefu'
O' Whisky Baba!

Two Triolets for Martine Nouet

POEMS • TRIOLETS

I

Some people say Martine Nouet
Is a wonderful whisky cook
Perhaps she deserves a triolet
Some people say Martine Nouet
Is the finest in the world today
And she's published an excellent book
Some of us say Martine Nouet
Is a wonderful whisky cook

II

Martine is the dude for whisky and food
Pure harmony and balance on a plate
I've met quite a few and I have to conclude
Martine is the dude for whisky and food
You think of the Louvre; a clever étude
Such is the art that she seeks to create
Martine is the dude for whisky and food
Pure harmony and balance on a plate

Martine is a journalist, originally from Paris, who now lives on Islay. She is a woman who follows her heart and once she realised that the subject she liked most to write about was whisky, she moved to the centre of the whisky universe — Islay.

She is an expert on food and an expert on whisky, but is probably most happy when she is able to combine those two passions; she creates whisky dinners, teaches courses, advises and writes about it, most notably in her wonderful book à table: whisky from glass to plate.

Years ago, while still living in France, she organised an annual Whisky Festival in Paris — I have many happy memories of attending this event on various occasions, usually with Jim McEwan and Norma Munro, a fine singer who lived on Islay at that time. One February, the event became a festival of whisky, food and love. Why has this winning combination never been repeated? I think I see a gap in the market.

Ideas for a Scotch Whisky Dinner

POEM

Cockaleekie and Cullen Skink
Roast Scotch lamb – nice and pink
Served wi' breid – plain or pan
A' wash'd doon wi' a tasty dram

Skirlie, kippers and Partan Bree
Come awa' in – you'll have had your tea
Sit doon Rab Ha – yer just the man
Grab a plate and a puckle dram

Bannocks, bridies and a wee Scotch Pie
Trooties and Squatties – steamed or
    fried
Come oan noo – tuck in tae the scran
And wash it doon wi' a tasty dram

Sugary shortbread petticoat tails
Hawick Balls and Jeddart Snails
Fatt'nin'? – Ah don't gie a tinker's damn
Just wash it doon wi' a tasty dram

Dundee Cake and Edinburgh Rock
Crappit Heids and Shooglie Jock
Dinna be shy tae pit oot yer hand
And wash it doon wi' a tasty dram

Stornoway Black and Lanark Blue
Macaroon Bars and Irn Bru
Then pokey hats fi the ice-cream van
Or wid ye raither hae anither dram?

Arbroath Smokies and Finnan Haddie
Porridge maks a good strong laddie
So stick yer spurtle in ma porridge pan
And then we'll hae anither dram

Clapshot, Stovies and Rumbledethumps
Atholl Brose and pineapple humps
Dinna be such a slaister, man
I'll fetch ye ower a tasty dram

Aberdeen Butteries and tattie scones
Oatcakes wi' some Caboc on
Get stuck in till ye canna stand
Then sit doon for a tasty dram

Serve up haggis, neeps and tatties
Deep fried Mars Bars for the fatties
Ye'll maybe need an oral exam
Or rinse yer mooth wi' a tasty dram

Clootie Dumplin' and Cabbie Claw
Soor Plooms and Stripped Baws
Sweets and gundy by the kilogram
And a wee shot glass o' a tasty dram

Scotch Broth, Buckies and black bun
Makin' tablet is muckle fun
A' the fare o' this fair land
And don't forget the tasty wee dram

Collops, Crowdie and a few Scotch Eggs
Tunnocks mak Tea Cakes and Caramel Logs
Eat till ye damage yer diaphragm
Then hae a wee painkiller dram

Berwick Cockles and Coulter's Candy
Grannie's Sookers are ayeways handy
Barley Sugars are in demand
And barley bree – aye, that's a dram

Mealie Puddin's and a Square Slice roll
Powsowdie winkin' oot a bowl
So put yer gas at a peep, Madame
And settle doon wi' a tasty dram

Keiller's marmalade and Colcannon
A flaky wee bite o' hot-smoked salmon
Consume as much as ye possibly can
Then wash it doon wi' a tasty dram

*

Cockaleekie	soup made with chicken and leeks
Cullen Skink	a milky fish soup containing smoked haddock, potatoes and onions
Skirlie	oatmeal fried with fat, onions and seasoning
Partan Bree	a soup featuring crab, and usually rice
Rab Ha	Robert Hall, a vagrant, known as the Glasgow Glutton; famous for his enormous capacity for eating
Trooties	trout
Squatties	squat lobster tails
Hawick Balls	hard boiled sweets
Jeddart Snails	(or Jethart Snails) – dark hard toffee sweets from Jedburgh
Cappit Heids	boiled fish heads stuffed with oats, suet and liver
Shooglie Jock	brawn in jelly

Stornoway Black	black pudding from Stornoway
Lanark Blue	an artisanal sheep's milk blue cheese made near Lanark
Pokey Hats	ice-cream cones
Arbroath Smokies	a type of hot-smoked haddock
Finnan Haddie	a type of cold-smoked haddock
Clapshot	mashed potatoes and turnips
Stovies	a dish of potatoes, onions and leftover meat
Rumbledethumps	a dish from the Scottish Borders – potato, cabbage and onion
Pineapple Humps	a Glasgow name for individual iced pineapple tarts
Aberdeen Butteries	bread rolls with a high lard content, also known as rowies
Caboc	a soft cream cheese log rolled in pinhead oatmeal
Clootie Dumplin'	a dried fruit and suet dumpling wrapped in a cloth and simmered
Cabbie Claw	a fish dish from the North-east using fish (often cod), parsley, horseradish and potato
Soor Plooms	round green boiled sweets with a sharp flavour – plooms are plums
Stripped Baws	black and white striped, round boiled sweets, with a minty flavour
Gundy	toffee
Buckies	winkles or small whelks
Black Bun	a spicy, dense, dark fruit cake wrapped in pastry
Collops	thin slices of meat mixed with onions, suet and seasoning
Crowdie	low-fat fresh cheese, said to alleviate the effects of whisky drinking!
Scotch Egg	boiled egg wrapped in sausage-meat, then bread-crumbed and deep fried
Berwick Cockles	soft, crumbly, mint-flavoured candies, with red stripes

Coulter's Candy	aniseed-flavoured sweets made famous in a children's song
Grannie's Sookers	pan drops (peppermint sweets)
Mealie Puddin'	a sausage shaped white pudding made of oatmeal and fat
Square Slice	Lorne sausage (sausage meat in a loaf shape – sliced and fried)
Powsowdie	sheep's head broth
Colcannon	originally from Ireland – but basically a version of bubble and squeak (re-fried cabbage, potato and onion)

Personally, I think wine goes better with food than whisky, but I have had some really memorable whisky dinners and they do work well, if prepared thoughtfully and skilfully. Martine Nouet is a class act in this department. The team at Freihardt restaurant in Heroldsberg, near Nuremberg are also great and the Taster Menu at the Queen Street restaurant of the Scotch Malt Whisky Society in Edinburgh are also great. The poem is a list of Scottish food items – though there seems to be a preponderance of potatoes, offal and sugary things – what does that say about our diet? But actually, our native produce – Scotch lamb, salmon, seafood, venison and Aberdeen Angus or Highland beef are second to none – I think I would stick to that, rather than powsowdie, crappit heids and shooglie Jock.

Songs

O thou, my MUSE! guid auld SCOTCH DRINK!
Whether thro' wimplin worms thou jink,
Or, richly brown, ream owre the brink,
In glorious faem,
Inspire me, till I lisp an' wink,
To sing thy name!

ROBERT BURNS; 'SCOTCH DRINK'

V

The Best Drink in the World

Distillation – Maturation – Evaporation – Inspiration.

More Than Just a Dram
The Barley Bree
Whisky for Breakfast
Whisky and Death
Special Sipping Whisky
Slow as Molasses
World of Whisky
The Wintertime is Coming

More Than Just a Dram

SONG • RECORDED ON THE ANGELS' SHARE • CDTRAX137

Take clear water from the hill
And barley from the lowlands,
Take a master craftsman's skill
And something harder to define,
Like secrets in the shape of copper stills
Or the slow, silent, magic work of time.

Whisky, you're the Devil in disguise,
At least to some that's the way it seems,
But you're more like an angel in my eyes,
Catch the heady vapours as they rise
And turn them into dreams.

Bring home sherry casks from Spain,
Sanlucar de Barrameda,
And fill them up again
With the spirit of the land.
Then let the wood work to the spirit's gain
In a process no-one fully understands.

Whisky you're...

Now the spirit starts out clear
But see the transformation
After many patient years
When at last the tale unfolds,
For the colours of the seasons will appear,
From palest yellow to the deepest gold.

Whisky you're...

When you hold it in your hand
It's the pulse of one small nation;
So much more than just a dram,
You can see it if you will –
The people and the weather and the land,
The past into the present is distilled.

Whisky, you're the Devil in disguise,
At least to some that's the way it seems,
But you're more like an angel in my eyes,
Catch the heady vapours as they rise,
And turn them into peaceful, pleasant dreams.

This was the first whisky song I ever wrote – started on Islay and finished on the Isle of Eigg (some islands don't make whisky, but they sure do drink it). It kind of sums up why I am passionate about whisky, while the chorus hints at the ambivalence to our national drink (or any alcoholic drink) that is never too far below the surface in Scotland.

The Barley Bree

SONG • TUNE – FAREWELL TO WHISKY (NIEL GOW)

When friends are gathered and the crack is bright
And talk and laughter echo through the night
Open a bottle for your joy and your delight
There's nothing better than the barley bree.

The barley bree, the barley bree
I had it first at my mother's knee
And since that time it's been a friend to me
Oh life is better wi' the barley bree

When it's cold and dark and snow is flying fast
And the long day's over and you're home at last
Warm up your spirit wi' the flame inside a glass
And a wee sensation o' the barley bree

The barley bree, the barley bree…

This life is difficult and hard at times
And your dreams get hammered by the daily grind
Forget aboot pick-me-ups and pills and tonic wines
And reach for a bottle o' the barley bree

The barley bree, the barley bree…

When God decides at last my soul to take
And I go on the journey that we all must make
I know that mine will be the happiest of wakes
If they toast my passing wi' the barley bree

The barley bree, the barley bree…

Apparently the British government prohibited the making of whisky in Scotland in 1799, on account of the failed barley harvest that year. The thought of a year without whisky being made was inspiration for a lament from Niel Gow, who was rather well known for his love of a good dram. He later composed a much merrier tune called 'Whisky, Welcome Back Again'.

I thought the tune deserved some new lyrics but I couldn't think of a reason to lament whisky (other than the price, maybe) so I lapsed into my default mode of positive appreciation.

Whisky for Breakfast

SONG • RECORDED ON WHISKY FOR BREAKFAST • CDTRAX361

I take whisky for my breakfast
To see me through the day
Just one little whisky
Helps me on my way
It clears my tubes, thins my blood
Clarifies my head
Just one little whisky
Then I go back to bed

I don't need no scrambled eggs
I don't need no bacon
A single malt is all I need
To stop my hands from shakin'

Some folks love their cornflakes
And others porridge oats
Shredded wheat, sugar puffs
Whatever floats your boat
If I have to eat grass for breakfast
This is the kind I'll choose
A little bit of barley
Converted into booze

I don't need no scrambled eggs...

I come from the land of Calvin
The Devil and John Knox
Winter lasts for half a year
And we sleep in woolly socks
If I lived in southern lands
And woke up in the sun
I wouldn't need breakfast whisky
Well, maybe just the one!

I don't need no scrambled eggs...

Claudio Bernasconi
Lives in St Moritz
He cleans his teeth with whisky
He very seldom spits
He brushes, then he gargles
And swallows it with glee
And then comes down for breakfast
And he has the same as me

I don't need no scrambled eggs...

When I go to Dufftown
I stay at the Tannochbrae
And Alan keeps some whisky
In an aerosol spray
He spreads a mist of whisky
Over my beans on toast
Then he squirts some on my tongue
And I like that the most!

When I go to Islay
I party all night long
Fun and drams and stories
And even the occasional song
Sometimes I take breakfast
Before I go to bed
But if there's nothing in the fridge
I have another dram instead

I don't need no scrambled eggs
I don't need no bacon
A single malt is all I need
To stop my hands from shakin'
To stop my knees from quakin'
To stop my bones from achin'
To stop my skin from flakin'
To stop my heart from breakin'
And unless I am mistaken'
I'll be dancing like a Jamaican
Oh, whisky for my breakfast
And I'm limbo dancing all day long

This is a song that I often adapt for different situations — adding verses about places or people on my travels. I have always believed that whisky, like champagne, is such a versatile drink that it can be enjoyed any time, any place. I confess that I have occasionally had whisky in the morning, sometimes with breakfast, sometimes with brunch sometimes just to celebrate being alive; but I can't imagine drinking beer, cider, wine or gin at breakfast time. I attended Martine Nouet's whisky festival in Paris a few times and once we headed off to a chateau in Normandy on the Saturday night and we were treated to a Sunday morning whisky brunch, that somehow morphed into an all afternoon session — happy days!

But let's be clear about this, once in a while is OK, but if you have whisky for breakfast most days — then you probably have a problem and should seek help, take up a hobby, or get a life.

After hearing this song, Alan Greune-Smith added an item to the breakfast menu at the Tannochbrae guest house in Dufftown (a highly recommended establishment) — 'Misty Beans' — people actually order it. The spray of whisky on the tongue is optional.

Whisky and Death

SONG • RECORDED ON WHISKY AND DEATH • FW001CD

When I die lay me in my grave
In a coffin made out of barrel staves
I could face eternity after I croak
In a box made of whisky-soaked oak

Say goodbye to me with a wake
After you make sure there's no mistake
Lay all my whiskies out in a line
And drink to me one last time

When I get to St Peter's gate
I'll dress up nice and I won't be late
I guess I won't have too long to wait
Because everyone else in the line
Will smell of the vault and the tomb
But the angels' eyes will shimmer and
    shine
When they smell my malt perfume

All my life I followed one rule
Be good, be cool, don't act the fool
And the best reward for a hard-
    working man
Is a decent dram in your hand

After death – if you hear from me
Que pasa hombre – Aaieee I'm a
    zombie
Don't run away – grab a whisky instead
And smash it over my head

Come on Death then where is thy
    sting?
Where are your demons with the torn
    black wings?
Carmina Burana let everyone sing
I'll look you in the eye
Though you're colder than Lady
    MacBeth
We're scared to live when we're scared
    to die
I'll take whisky and death

Take me to the far side
Take me to the dark side
Let me feel the edge of the knife
I see a pale horse
And a fiery cross
So take me to the water
Take me to the water
Take me to the water of life

You prowl in the dark with your crows and cats
Your red-eyed rats and your graveyard bats
But I pour a dram on the blackest night
And it shines with a golden light

The universe is cold and vast
So raise a glass to me after I've passed
Life is short as a Disney cartoon
You know your turn will come soon

Come on Death then where is thy sting?
Where are your demons with the torn black wings?
Carmina Burana let everyone sing
I'll look you in the eye
Though you're colder than Lady MacBeth
We're scared to live when we're scared to die
I'll take whisky and death

This song started off as a bit of a fantasy about having a coffin made out of whisky barrels; if they can be used for garden furniture, plant pots, candle holders etc. — why not? Then it got even more silly — but in the end I used it as the title track for the CD — it seemed a natural progression from the previous CD Whisky for Breakfast.

Special Sipping Whisky

SONG • RECORDED ON WHISKY FOR BREAKFAST • CDTRAX361

The sun is going down
And the barbeque is on
My friends are coming round
We'll stay up till the dawn
It's Friday evening
And the working day is done
It's time to open the whisky

Now everybody's here
And I've got some music on
There's ice for the beer
And candles on the lawn
The moon is coming up
And the sun will soon be gone
It's time to open the whisky

Not just any old whisky will do
It's got to be something special for you
For you are my friend and I'll give you your due
And pour you a special sipping whisky

So how about this one
It's twenty-nine-years old
The colour is a blissful
Burgundy gold
Just give it time
For the magic to unfold
Another fine special sipping whisky

It doesn't need soda
It doesn't need ice
Don't mix it with cola
That would not be nice
There's fruit and flowers
And honey and spice
In this special sipping whisky

Not just any old whisky will do
It's got to be something special for you
For you are my friend and I'll give you your due
And pour you a special sipping whisky

If you appreciate whisky
You'll appreciate friends
That's how it hits me
It seems to make sense
Old friends, bookends
Single malts or blends
Special friends need special whisky

Keep all the cheap stuff for the rest of the pack
They might be happy with Johnnie or Jack
They're glugging it, they're slugging it, they're
*   knocking it back*
We'll stick to special sipping whisky

Keep all the cheap stuff for your unwanted guests
Or rub it on your chest if you've got pests in your vest
For cooking or cocktails it might just pass the test
Or give it to the school tombola

Good whisky can be quite expensive and I won't usually spend much on the stuff I drink at home alone — but when close and valued friends come round, that's another matter. Good whisky, whether that's just an unusually tasty dram or something old, or something rare, stimulates the conversation and enhances bonding — so for anything from after dinner occasions to bothy nights, it is sometimes worth paying a bit extra — though how much might depend on who is in the company!

Slow as Molasses

SONG • RECORDED ON WHISKY AND DEATH • FW001CD

Slow as molasses — a glacial pace
Slow as the lines etched by time on your face
Slow as two continents drift apart
Slow as the healing of a broken heart

Time is a healer — that's the simple truth
The wisdom of age is paid by the folly of youth
Time takes no prisoners, takes no heed
And it goes so slow when you've a need for speed

Baby it takes time
There's no other way
If you want to see that firefly shine
You have to wait till the close of day

We do what we have to with power and heat
To get from the barley something charmingly sweet
But then the best thing that we can do
Is to let the years slowly trickle through

There's a rhythm of living that we're wise to keep
We work and we play all the day — and then we sleep
Whisky too has its day and its night
And the more it sleeps the more it gives delight

Baby it takes time
There's no other way
Nobody said it was a crime
To keep something back for a rainy day

So savour the memory of all that's passed
Think of the whisky as history in a glass
Let your mind drift to way back when —
Was your life any sweeter then?

Baby it takes time
There's no other way
You can find that elusive rhyme
Don't be content with a bent cliché.

Slow as molasses — a glacial pace
Slow as the lines etched by time on your face
Slow as two continents drift apart
Slow as the healing of a broken heart

The older the whisky, generally the more expensive it is — but is it always worth the premium? In terms of the aroma and the taste — well, usually, but not always and in terms of the alcoholic kick if that's what you are looking for — well, usually not, as the alcoholic strength mostly reduces with age. However, there are some other reasons to appreciate older whiskies; firstly, age often gives to whisky a character that is difficult to describe — it's like the patina on an old piece of wooden furniture — the oak, if it hasn't overpowered the spirit, gives something very subtle to it — an extra layer of depth and complexity, a certain je ne sais quoi. Secondly, whisky making techniques have changed over the years and it is often interesting to compare today's efforts with those of the 1950s or 1960s. But most importantly there is the emotional element — when you share a good bottle of 25 or 30 year old malt with a friend, you usually start talking and reflecting about the changes that have happened in the world or in your lives since that whisky was made — memories, whether happy or sad, are nonetheless emotional. This is something you just don't get with gin, for all its reputation for stirring up emotions. In summary, it usually is worth waiting for and worth paying for.

World of Whisky

SONG • RECORDED ON ONE FOR THE ROAD • CDTRAX313

From the Lowlands to the Highlands
From Japan to the Hebrides
From Orkney to Kentucky
And the far Antipodes
From Tennessee to Canada
And Ireland's emerald land
There's a world of whisky out there
So let's have another dram
There's a world of whisky out there
So let's have another dram

Here's to the corn and the maize
The barley and the rye
Here's to the good old angels
Floating up on high
Here's to the worms and the washbacks
The still house and the vats
And the wood so tight – a lovely sight
Hoggies and big butts

It's better for you than red wine
Less calories than beer
You can drink it any time of day
And any time of year
You can pour it on your porridge
Or dab it behind your ears
In the hallowed halls of alcohol
Whisky has no peer

From the Lowlands to the Highlands...

Here's to the guys who drink the stuff
A little or a lot
And here's to the guys who sell it to 'em
What a difficult job they've got
Here's to the whisky blenders
May their noses be insured
But the guys who make it — you can take it
The keys to heaven are yours

From the Lowlands to the Highlands...

Whisky for the heart
Whisky for the soul
Whisky stands for friendship
And stories to be told
And all around the world
Whenever whisky's poured
The hatred of the past will end at last
And peace can be restored

From the Lowlands to the Highlands...

This song was written in response to a request from Whisky Magazine *for me to compose them 'an anthem'. I did the best I could, though it is far from an anthem. It does try to reflect their mission statement of 'celebrating the whiskies of the world'. Appropriately, it was first performed in Tokyo when I attended my first Whisky Live event in Japan — lots of Japanese whisky drinkers singing along, struggling with the chorus, but eventually joining in enthusiastically with the last line — 'Let's have another dram!'*

These days every country in the world seems to be making whisky (someone told me there are more whisky distilleries in Germany now than in Scotland) — and some of them are making a reasonable job of it. However, by any measure, at least for now, Scotland remains pre-eminent in the world of whisky and, for a small country, that's something to be proud of.

The Wintertime is Coming

SONG • TUNE – WILD MOUNTAIN THYME

Oh the wintertime is coming
And not a thing is blooming
And when this storm has passed us
There's another cold front looming

Bringing snow, bloody snow
Rain and windy weather
For nine months every year
You get no rest whatsoever
From the snow, bloody snow.

Oh the wintertime is coming
No more croissants and brioches
At the city pavement cafes
Noo it's porridge and galoshes

In the snow, bloody snow...

If my true love was a duck
Or a polar bear or penguin
Maybe she'd have stuck
Around – tae see a happy ending

Tae the snow, bloody snow...

Oh the wintertime is coming
We will need oor central heating
And a wee drap o' whisky
Just keep your auld heart beating

In the snow, bloody snow...

Oh the wintertime is coming
And oor country is benighted
Just hae a drammie handy
And keep the log fire lighted

In the snow, bloody snow...

Oh the wintertime is coming
When oor hooses are like fridges
And the only consolation
Is you don't get bloody midges

In the snow, bloody snow
Rain and windy weather
But you'll no hear me complainin'
For my lips are froze together
In the snow, bloody snow.

Whisky – Scotland's answer to central heating and the only thing that keeps us going during the long, cold, dark and dreary winter months up here. Why are the whisky festivals in the summer? Surely they should be in the winter – in fact the whole winter should be a three month long whisky festival, starting on Saint Andrew's Day – then December, January and February would pass in the twinkling of an eye!

VI

These are a few of my favourite drams

I usually say my favourite whisky is the next one – but...

Talisker Bay
Macallan
A'bunadh
The Arran Dram
A Turquoise Frame of Mind
The Bruichladdich Dram
Black Art

Talisker Bay

SONG • RECORDED ON WHISKY FOR BREAKFAST • CDTRAX361

I picked up stones on Talisker Bay
I threw them in the sea
I had to find a different way
Something right for me

I watched the boats go sailing by
I saw the waterfall
Dropping down the cliff so high
I heard the seabirds call

I felt the waves on Talisker Bay
Crashing over the stones
The ancient dance of foam and spray
And tall ships coming home

I threw my voice across the sky
It fell into the sea
I was Icarus flying high
Nobody watching me

And time stood still for me
Tasting the smoke and the stone

I poured a dram on Talisker Bay
The night time coming on
I decided I would stay
And feel the kiss of dawn

A driftwood fire to keep me warm
A liquid fire inside
And suddenly the inner storm
Quietened down and died

And time stood still for me
Tasting the smoke and the stone
By the margin of the sea
Sweet salty memories of home

Beneath the stars on Talisker Bay
I sang a simple song
And all the world seemed far away,
The night still and long

Something in that Talisker dram
Opened up my eyes
I came close to understanding
The things that I should prize
That doesn't make me wise

But time stood still for me
Tasting the smoke and the stone
By the margin of the sea
Sweet salty memories
Sweet salty memories of home

Once upon a time, working in the cocktail bar of the Arisaig Hotel, I began to get interested in single malts and would often recommend Talisker to customers, as it was a dram that was made not far away and somehow reflected the character of the west coast like no other. To my taste the Talisker 100 proof was incomparable and it became my favourite whisky for a long time.

Many years later, while working on a website account of visiting all the west coast distilleries for an organisation called The Whisky Coast, I called in at Talisker and had a chat with the distillery manager. He gave me a bottle of Talisker 10 year old as I was leaving and I took it over to Talisker Bay. That is a wild, atmospheric place – perhaps the real spiritual home of Talisker single malt. The right whisky, in the right place, at the right time, can change your life – and that's what this song is about – whisky as epiphany!

Macallan

SONG • RECORDED ON WHISKY FOR BREAKFAST • CDTRAX361

The mountain stands before you
There's a valley in between
This spirit can restore you
It's the finest I have seen
With my own eyes
With my own eyes
And there's a river running by
Oh, forever, running by
Macallan hello
Macallan you and I
And away down below
There's a river running by

Time is like a river
Life is like a dream
If I let the spirit take me
I can see up the stream
With my own eyes
With my own eyes
And there's a river running by
Oh, forever, running by
Macallan I know
Macallan I try
And away down below
There's a river running by

I have seen the barrels
That hold the spirit rolled
Beside the fields of barley
The shining fields of gold
With my own eyes
With my own eyes
And there's a river running by
Oh, forever, running by
Macallan I glow
Macallan I cry
And away down below
There's a river running by

Sunshine falls like honey
Stars are diamond rings
Sometimes I see rainbows
And even angels' wings
With my own eyes
With my own eyes
And there's a river running by
Oh, forever, running by
Macallan bravo
Macallan fly high
And away down below
There's a river running by

Under the water, sunlight on sand
Just like the light that shines
Through the glass that sits in my hand

Macallan is a quintessential Speyside distillery. It is in the heart of Speyside and lies closer to the river than most of the others and indeed has a fishing hut on the river bank. Looking out from the still house you don't actually see the river; you see the land above the far bank, rising all the way up to the summit of Ben Rinnes, but you know it is there.

I was invited to perform at a Burns Supper in the distillery a few years ago and wrote the song for that occasion.

A'bunadh

SONG • RECORDED ON ONE FOR THE ROAD • CDTRAX313

I love you A'bunadh
You take me away
Winter storms may be howling –
I can feel the warm breath of May
It's a sunny day

I love you A'bunadh
In you I can hear
The rhythmic pounding of the dancers
Raising dust in a bar in Sevilla
And I love the way that feels

Like the words of a poet that's long been dead
You're swimming around and around in my head
Like the words of a song still to be sung
You're there, right there
On the tip of my tongue

I love you A'bunadh
Through you I can see
The golden glow from the dawn of the world
And I feel it shining on me
Endlessly

Like the words...

I love you A'bunadh
You speak to my heart
Caught up in the spin of life's tumble
You whisper me back to the start
And I need that

Like the words…

James Fleming built the Aberlour Distillery in 1879. He turned out to be quite a benefactor for the town and is still respected and remembered there. The distillery released a special whisky called A'bunadh in 1997 as a tribute to him. The name means 'the original' and the style was intended to reflect the kind of whisky Fleming would have produced — natural strength, no age statement, non chill-filtered and matured in Oloroso casks. That original batch was so popular that there have now been more than 50 batches made — it remains one of the best value single malts in Scotland. Drinking it, I often reflect on the magical marriage of flavours that arises from Scottish barley-derived spirit maturing in wine casks from Andalucia. This song came out of such reflections and the music has a nod in the direction of Spain.

The Arran Dram

SONG • RECORDED ON WHISKY FOR BREAKFAST • CDTRAX361

Watch the eagles fly
Over waterfalls
See the bright moon rise
Where the seabirds call
And the clear night skies
Are so deep and wide
It all makes you feel so small

When the long walk's done
Leave the hill behind
Hear the river run
Through the fragrant pines
And when the smiling sun
And his friendly face have gone
Something inside still shines

In a troubled life
You need a sense of calm
And a just reward for doing all you can
So every busy woman
And every hard-pressed man
Can see their place in the master plan
Through the twinkling lights
And the starry nights
That you find in the Arran dram

When the whispering sea
Seems to call you home
And the only place to be
Is on the shore all alone
Let your spirit sail free
Through the salt sea spray
Like a bird up above a standing stone

In a troubled life
You need a sense of calm
And a just reward for doing all you can
So every busy woman
And every hard-pressed man
Can see their place in the master plan
Through the shimmering lights
And the silken nights
That you find in the Arran dram

When the night's long veil
Has been pulled aside
And the dawn so pale
Grows bright and wide
And the great Goat Fell
Like some high, Holy Grail
Burns like a beacon on the Clyde

In a troubled life
You need a sense of calm
And a just reward for doing all you can
So every busy woman
And every hard-pressed man
Can see their place in the master plan
Through the ice-bright lights
And the hot summer nights
That you find in the Arran dram

Oooh we will meet there far across the sea
Oooh we will walk where eagles fly free
Oooh we will talk over many drams
And we will hold gold in our hands

The first thing you see entering the visitor centre at Arran Distillery in Lochranza is a fake waterfall and two golden eagles on the wall above it. The distillery has a bit of a relationship with the golden eagles that live in the mountains behind it — they tend to make an appearance on special occasions.

It is a privileged experience to enjoy a single malt near or at the place of its creation — especially when that place is worthy of a pilgrimage, as the Isle of Arran undoubtedly is.

The chorus of this song also has something of my philosophy about drinking whisky — it is best enjoyed as a reward for having done something and if you give it your full attention it can evoke many things in the memory and imagination.

A Turquoise Frame of Mind

SONG • RECORDED ON WHISKY FOR BREAKFAST • CDTRAX361

It's been a long hard day
I've earned my pay
And now I'm trying to unwind
And now I know
What I must do
I'm in a turquoise frame of mind

The sky is black
Beyond the blue
But if you could look behind
I know that you
Just like me
Would find a turquoise frame of mind

It's the colour of sunshine
Through a shallow sea
It's the colour of love, baby
Protecting me
And when I go to Heaven, if I do
I know I'll find
All the angels sitting around
In a turquoise frame of mind

All those Kings
And all those Queens
Way back through the mists of time
With all their slaves
And precious things
They had a turquoise frame of mind

But I've got you
And I've got this
And I'm still heading down the line
The simple pleasure
Of a kiss
And a turquoise frame of mind

It's the colour of sunshine...

Old Shylock's girl
She sold his ring
And it nearly drove him blind
She got a monkey
But he just lost
His turquoise frame of mind

The sky is black
Beyond the blue
But if you could look behind
I know that you
Just like me
Would find a turquoise frame of mind

It's the colour of sunshine...

Bruichladdich chose turquoise as their corporate colour quite early on after the re-opening of the distillery in 2001. The colour on the packaging can be quite striking, which is a definite advantage when competing with other brands on the shop shelf. However, they claimed that the colour was chosen because it reflected the colour of the sea, just outside the distillery gates, on Loch Indaal. Mark Reynier felt vindicated when he read subsequently that some scientists had discovered that the true colour of the cosmos is — turquoise! Yeah, right — but it gave me the idea for this song.

The Bruichladdich Dram

SONG • RECORDED ON WHISKY FOR BREAKFAST • CDTRAX361

When you wake up in the morning and you're just feeling crap
Wi' fits or faints or fevers – don't get into a flap
For tinnitus or shingles or a lack of inner calm
The cure is in a bottle of the Bruichladdich dram

The Bruichladdich dram, the Bruichladdich dram
The cure is in a bottle of the Bruichladdich dram

When life isn't turning out the way you'd always planned
The people that you work with are like the Ku Klux Klan
The kids are bad, the wife is mad and nags ad nauseam
The chances are you need a little Bruichladdich dram

The Bruichladdich dram, the Bruichladdich dram
The chances are you need a little Bruichladdich dram

When you're shuffling on your zimmer frame and thinking of the past
And the little time that's left seems to disappear so fast
Don't just sit there waiting for that Royal telegram
Just wrap your stiff old fingers round a Bruichladdich dram

The Bruichladdich dram, the Bruichladdich dram
Just wrap your stiff old fingers round a Bruichladdich dram

When you want to celebrate – no matter what the cause
You've done something great and deserved the applause
Your numbers have come up or you've passed a big exam
Don't pop the old champagne – but pop the Bruichladdich dram

The Bruichladdich dram, the Bruichladdich dram
Don't pop the old champagne — pop the Bruichladdich dram

Now Jim has made a whisky and he calls it his Black Art
It's mystical, it's magical — bewitches the heart
Soon every lass on Islay will have to buy a pram
Don't blame Islay cheese — blame the Bruichladdich dram

The Bruichladdich dram, the Bruichladdich dram
Don't blame Islay cheese — blame the Bruichladdich dram

When you're far away from Islay and wishing you were there
There's little point in fretting and pulling out your hair
A book of Whisky Legends and a CD by the Man
Kick off your shoes and pour yourself a Bruichladdich dram

The Bruichladdich dram, the Bruichladdich dram
Kick off your shoes and pour yourself a Bruichladdich dram

We all know that whisky is medicinal — and so it stands to reason that good whisky is very medicinal. We've known since Holinshed's Chronicles (1577) *that whisky can cure, heal, fix and improve almost everything in life — the text is now printed on a wall at Lindores Abbey Distillery, but can also be easily found on the internet — and is worth a read.*

My claims for the positive effects of Bruichladdich single malt are far from exaggerated — try it! The reference to Islay cheese comes from the well-known fact that its import into Italy was once banned by the Pope because of its considerable aphrodisiac effect on those who ate it; at least that's what they say on Islay. The full story can be found in my book Whisky Legends of Islay.

Black Art

SONG • RECORDED ON WHISKY FOR BREAKFAST • CDTRAX361

With your strange black art
My defences fall apart
You can feed upon my heart
I can't resist it

Come the twilight time
I can lose my mind
It's pierced through by signs
That change and twist it

Life is but a dream
And dreams are only dreams —
Or so some Spanish poet said
But when you come along
My life becomes a song
A beautiful song inside my head
A beautiful song in my head

There's a deep black hole
Where the Devil's in control
He tries to win my soul
And he is heartless

But though it burns my lip
If I only take a sip
I know I will not slip
Into the darkness

Life is but a dream…

There's a sleek black cat
In a tall black hat
And he turns me to a rat
So he can chase me

But I do not need to hide
There's an angel by my side
She spreads her wings out wide
And he can't face me

Life is but a dream…

In the deep black night
With no starlight
Owls take to flight
In slow motion

But the Scorpio moon
Will rise above the dunes
And shine on Jim McEwan
Making potions

Life is but a dream
And dreams are only dreams —
Or so some Spanish poet said
But when you come along
My life becomes a song
A beautiful song inside my head
A beautiful song in my head
A beautiful song in my head

One of my favourite Bruichladdich expressions is the Black Art. It is just so spot on — the whisky and the packaging are both very sexy. Jim McEwan was always very secretive about which casks it had been matured in. For the 5th edition, Adam Hannett is continuing this secrecy. It all gives the dram a certain mystery — it is a very tasty enigma — and so my song tried to reflect this. The Spanish poet referred to is Calderon de la Barca — 'toda la vida es sueño, y los sueños, sueños son': all life is a dream, and dreams are only dreams.

VII

Whisky Heroes

The story of whisky making (and whisky selling) is littered with heroes (both sung and un-sung), larger than life characters and all round good guys – and increasingly, women.

> All the Whisky Men
> Old Minmore
> Elijah Craig
> Paul Campbell
> Magic Ship of Dreams
> The Boys at Bruichladdich
> Pestering Jim

All the Whisky Men

SONG • RECORDED ON WHISKY AND DEATH • FW001CD

I poured a dram and I closed my eyes
I'm in a room with the whisky men
All those cool and colourful guys
From nowadays to way back when
Five hundred years of the Whisky Men
Heroes and characters one and all
From monacled Johnny and Charlie MacLean
To Friar John Cor and his famous eight bolls

All the whisky men
I'm in their company
All the Whisky Men
Having a dram with me

Tommy Dewar's burning my ears
With all the tales of his latest trip
Old Glenlivet's just appeared
Packing two pistols on his hip
Long John's longer than little John Black
But he's not blacker than old Long John
Jim McEwan never holds back
His wonderful stories rolling on and on

All the whisky men...

Bernasconi has the biggest whisky bar
Two and a half thousand to be precise
Gunter Sommer has the smallest by far
No beer, no vodka, no wine, no dice
Richard Paterson in a very nice tie
Is throwing stuff around like he tends to do
Angels are teaching Michael Jackson to fly
He's a Yorkshire Lithuanian atheist Jew

All the whisky men...

Jim Murray's preaching from his bible again
And Restless Peter can't keep still
All the Grants are down from the Glen
Pip Hills is grilling Dr Bill
I see two guys who are having a row
Aeneas Coffey and Robert Stein
It's time to open some whisky now
Pour them a dram and they'll get along fine

All the whisky men...

Suddenly my dream goes Pop!
All the whisky men disappear
I didn't want that dream to stop
I'm softly sobbing in my beer
A door flies open with a sudden noise
Shrieks of laughter and bows and frills
Now I don't miss those whisky boys
I'm surrounded by the whisky girls

All the whisky girls

I'm in their company
All the whisky girls
Having a dram with me

All the whisky girls
I'm in their company
All the whisky girls
Laughing and teasing me

I find that inspiration often flows from a glass of single malt — the trick is to make your mind receptive and for me that usually works best when I am drinking alone and I drift into a kind of daydream or reverie. In this particular daydream I was having a dram with a few of the great names from the world of whisky, some that I really have worked with and some that are long gone. In the distant past most of the great names were men — but that is changing rapidly.

Old Minmore

SONG • RECORDED ON WHISKY FOR BREAKFAST • CDTRAX361

From the Ladder Hills to Drumin
Down by Tamnavoulin
The Livet tumbles on towards the Spey
But the river owes its glory
And its place in many story
To the man who lies beside it at Tombae

Old Minmore, Old Minmore
Though few would believe it
He could dream and achieve it
Smith o' Glenlivet, Old Minmore

In these quiet untamed hills
There were once a hundred stills
Hidden from the gaugers' prying eyes
The peasants and the squires
Saw smoke from whisky fires
Rise up unmolested to the skies

But the times were changing fast
And the old ways couldn't last
Though few could see the way that things would fall
One man seemed to know
The way the world would go
Smith could read the writing on the wall

Old Minmore, Old Minmore…

Smith found it much more risky
To make his legal whisky
For the smugglers in the Glen were mad as hell
They said he was a traitor
To creators o' the cratur
And they'd burn his place with him inside as well

But Smith was not the kind
To be forced to change his mind
And he always played the hand that he was dealt
So to keep his dream alive
Or simply to survive
He wore a pair of pistols in his belt

Old Minmore, Old Minmore...

Between the Livet and the Avon
The eagle and the raven
Are the only ones who see what deeds are done
They say courage never fails
And dead men tell no tales
Smith carried on with what he had begun

Old Minmore, Old Minmore...

The story of how George Smith took the significant step in 1824 to take out a licence to start making legal whisky (and the fact he had to wear a pair of pistols for protection) is a well known part of Speyside whisky lore. Those pistols are still on display at the Glenlivet visitor centre. There is something of the spirit of the Wild West in this story and there is still an untamed, upland feel about Glenlivet, even today – perhaps the most beautiful part of Speyside. My song tries to capture something of the cowboy ballad in its feel.

Near the distillery is the house called Minmore. For a while it was a restaurant and of course further back it was the residence of George Smith, and that is why his nickname in his later years was Old Minmore. His grave is at Tombae – that, and the grave of James Fleming at Aberlour, are worthy places of pilgrimage for lovers of Speyside malts.

Elijah Craig

SONG • RECORDED ON ONE FOR THE ROAD • CDTRAX313

Elijah Craig was a preacher man
He could save your soul from hell
And give you a taste of heaven
From his old corn whiskey still
Elijah Craig, he served us well

Elijah Craig had good strong hands
Confidence and skill
He took the river in an untamed land
And made it drive the mill
He always seemed the kind of man
Who would have a damn good try
And he turned out timber, rope and grain
For the pioneers to buy

Elijah Craig was a preacher man
He could save your soul from hell
And give you a taste of heaven
From his old corn whiskey still
Elijah Craig, he served us well

Elijah Craig had a good strong voice
It rang like a mission bell
His words rained down from cathedral skies
And they held you in their spell
And when he sang the holy psalms
It made your spirit rise
There was something special in this man
You could see it in his eyes

He took his place on the frontier
And he knew what to do
To ease the pain of the pilgrims passing through

Elijah Craig had a good business brain
And the soul of an engineer
His family came from a Highland glen
Out west to the new frontier
He preached the word of a vengeful God
And he strove to do his will
But somehow he knew God would smile
On his old corn whiskey still

Elijah Craig was a preacher man
He could save your soul from hell
And give you a taste of heaven
From his old corn whiskey still
Elijah Craig, he served us well

He took his place on the frontier
And he knew
Just what to do
For me and you
And all the pilgrims passing through
'Cos he knew
That we are all just pilgrims passing through

I was invited to play at the Kentucky Bourbon Festival by Heaven Hill Distillery. One of their brands is Elijah Craig bourbon – and it turns out that Elijah, one of the founding fathers of bourbon, had Scottish connections – his mother (or grandmother, sources differ) came from Craigellachie in Scotland. Certainly, when I read that he was an engineer, a Baptist preacher and he made whiskey, it all sounded very Scottish to me.

He is credited with the discovery that charring the inside of oak casks improves the flavour of the whiskey. This may have been accidental and fortuitous or it might have been down to experimentation and an enquiring mind, but it seemed his whiskey was considered superior by the discerning drinkers of New Orleans and as those barrels had the Bourbon stamp on them (from being shipped out of Bourbon County, though Elijah did not actually distil in Bourbon County) – so the cry went up for more 'Bourbon' and a legend and a brand was born and built upon.

Paul Campbell

SONG • RECORDED ON WHISKY FOR BREAKFAST • CDTRAX361

My name is Paul Campbell, I come from Balmichael
In the hills above Arran's western shore
My poor heart is grieving for Arran I am leaving
Just like my brother before
Away to the west I am flying in haste
And I fear I may not see Arran, evermore

The Government's agents, those parasitic gaugers
Have pestered this island for a year
They're ruthless and they're wicked and they killed Isa Nicholl
And left her poor children in tears
They come in the night and they break things for spite
And they think that the people will crumble, out of fear

They came to Balmichael when the still was at a trickle
And destroyed everything they could find
I couldn't hold my temper and though I don't remember
They say I made one of them blind
But a man has to fight when he thinks he is right
And if he loses all in the struggle, never mind

For striking my betters they put my hands in fetters
And sent me to Glasgow for trial
But the skipper was McArthur and close to Dumbarton
He spoke to me in Gaelic and he smiled
So I jumped overboard where the white breakers roared
For a Campbell will never be friendless in Argyll

In all kinds of weather I've been hiding in the heather
Just like a shadow unseen
But I know they will hunt me and I have to leave the country
It seems like the worst kind of dream
So I'm travelling on to where my brother has gone
And we'll see if the good folk take whisky in New Orleans

My name is Paul Campbell, I come from Balmichael…

Having written The Arran Dram (page 88) and having performed it a couple of times at the distillery, I was on the lookout for another subject as the distillery Managing Director at that time, Douglas Davidson, was interested in making a CD. In the old days, Arran was a hotbed of illicit whisky making, probably because of the proximity of a considerable market in Glasgow and the true story of Paul Campbell seemed perfect for a ballad. We did make a CD of six songs, called The Arran Dram, though that is no longer generally available.

It is interesting that Paul Campbell is another whisky maker from Scotland who ended up in the USA, probably making bourbon whisky, a bit like the story of Elijah Craig (page 103). As you can probably guess, Balmichael is pronounced Bal-mickle.

Magic Ship of Dreams

SONG • RECORDED ON WHISKY AND DEATH • FW001CD

Butts are bumping and barrels are bouncing
Hoggies are hammering along
All aboard the magic ship of dreams
Taking whisky down to Major Tom

His name is Thomas Ewers
And his crew are busy beavers
Working hard from noon till morn
He'll fix the shakes and fevers
Of the spiritual believers
They'll be pacified in Paderborn

Butts are bumping and barrels are bouncing…

He's got the Bunnahabhain
And he's got the Bruichladdich
Auchentoshan, Allt a Bhainne and Tamdhu
Ardmore, Bowmore,
Dalmore, Tormore
Any dram with 'more' will do.

Butts are bumping and barrels are bouncing…

When the wife is scowlin'
And the weans are howlin'
And everything you handle falls apart
Thomas is the fixer
And his magical elixir
Will kindle up the flame inside your heart.

Butts are bumping and barrels are bouncing...

In his warehouse shoppie
You can try a little droppie
Poured with a sympathetic smile
Let's raise a glass to Thomas
He delivers on his promise
And he'll always go the extra mile

Butts are bumping and barrels are bouncing...

He takes in deliveries
From dozens of distilleries
Nothing but the best for Tam the man
There's something of our history
And just a little mystery
In every single golden dram

Butts are bumping and barrels are bouncing...

Thomas Ewers from Paderborn in Germany has a whisky company called Malts of Scotland; he has won the Independent Bottlers Challenge at least three times, no easy thing for someone based outside of Scotland. He works extremely hard, he knows his whiskies and he cares passionately about quality. We have met many times and have become friends. The first time he created a Robin Laing bottling on his label, I asked if I could do anything in return. 'Write me a song' he said. I sat down and imagined all his wonderful whisky casks being shipped from Scotland to Germany and thought how I would like to be on board. Of course, casks don't actually get shipped out of Scotland — but that's poetic licence.

The Boys at Bruichladdich

SONG • TUNE – BOOZING, BLOODY WELL BOOZING

Who are the boys with the over-sized grins?
The boys at Bruichladdich
Who brought confidence back to the Rinns?
The boys at Bruichladdich
They've mastered the art of distilling with style
By not hesitating to go one more mile
And they make the best whisky from Carrick to Kyle
The boys at Bruichladdich

Bruichladdich simply the best
Bruichladdich impressed all the rest
We're blest in the west so let us ingest
A dram of Bruichladdich

Who should we ask to brew Islay beer?
The boys at Bruichladdich
Who should we contract to build the next pier?
The boys at Bruichladdich
When other distilleries run out of oil
In sheer desperation who will they call
For emergency rations of 'usquebaugh baul'?
The boys at Bruichladdich

Bruichladdich simply the best
Bruichladdich impressed all the rest
We're blest in the west so let us ingest
A dram of Bruichladdich

They might only fill 80 barrels a day
The boys at Bruichladdich
But who are the scourge of the SWA?
The boys at Bruichladdich
The big boys say they are everyone's friends
But they make up the rules for their own evil ends
But who knows the difference between malts and blends?
The boys at Bruichladdich

Bruichladdich simply the best
Bruichladdich impressed all the rest
We're blest in the west so let us ingest
A dram of Bruichladdich

Who is it keeps all the lads on the rails?
The girls at Bruichladdich
And sometimes they knock the wind
　　right oot their sails
The girls at Bruichladdich
There's Lynn and there's Lorna and
　　Ella as well
But they're no the worst – for I have
　　heard tell
That Barbara and Chrissie and Mary
　　give hell
Tae the boys at Bruichladdich

Bruichladdich simply the best
Bruichladdich impressed all the rest
We're blest in the west so let us ingest
A dram of Bruichladdich

> *Boozing, Bloody Well Boozing – a great song – I got it from a Hamish Imlach LP and it became a great joining in standard in the good old days when I sang in the Ensign Ewart pub in Edinburgh with Jim Knight and Colin Ramage.*
>
> *I used the tune to fashion this wee tribute to the staff at Bruichladdich Distillery. It reflects some of the issues and some of the personnel who were around at the time of writing – but things move on…*

Pestering Jim

SONG • TUNE – WESTERING HOME

I'm pestering Jim wi' a glass in my hand
Just one more story Jim – just one more dram
No-one can tell them the way that he can
He's a true legend of Islay

I've travelled to lands – both far and near
But nowhere to Islay at all can compare
It gladdens my heart – it's a joy to be here
With Jim McEwan on Islay

I'm pestering Jim wi' a glass in my hand...

Sing of the sunset the sea and the sand
Sing to the seals that come close to the land
Sing of the folk and the wonderful drams
With Jim McEwan on Islay

I'm pestering Jim wi' a glass in my hand...

Jim is the laddie that we love the best
He should have medals all over his chest
A man of his island – a man of the West
He's a true legend of Islay

I'm pestering Jim wi' a glass in my hand...

Jim we salute you and all that you've done
In the world of whisky, Jim – you are the one
And Islay is proud to call you her son
The cheekiest laddie on Islay

I'm pestering Jim wi' a glass in my hand...

So fill up your glasses — right to the brim
Let us all stand for a tribute to Jim
Calmac should name a boat after him
He's a true legend of Islay

I'm pestering Jim wi' a glass in my hand...

I've known Jim MacEwan since the late 1990s, when he was still working at Bowmore and my song Bruichladdich (page 134) was mainly written for him when he moved to that company in 2001. His contribution to the revitalisation of Bruichladdich Distillery and the Rinns of Islay has been immense. He has always been an Islay man first and foremost, no matter what company he was working for. When he announced he was retiring I started working on a tribute and could not think of a better tune than Westering Home which is a kind of Islay anthem. I don't think he likes the idea of praise or tributes, even though it is rather tongue in cheek, but I do mean it — so here it is, Jim — as a thank you for all the stories and all the drams!

VIII

Relationships

When it comes to relationships between men and women,
whisky is often the source of conflict – but not always!

Monkey Shoulder
Heaven Hill
Johnnie and Me
The Wee Cooper o' Fife
Ugly Betty
Whisky Widow

Monkey Shoulder

SONG • RECORDED ON WHISKY FOR BREAKFAST • CDTRAX361

I saw her standing there
Long black hair
Was it a snare
Or an answered prayer?
I wanted to hold her
Make my arms enfold her
Instead I just told her

Hey, you bring the ice
I've got the flame
You take the sweetness
I'll take the blame
If it smoulders

You've got the sunny smile
But I've got the Monkey Shoulder
Yeah, yeah, yeah, yeah,
The Monkey Shoulder

We could be Bonnie and Clyde
Jekyll and Hyde
Let's go for a ride
It's stuffy inside
And I wanted to kiss her
I just could not resist her
Then she said in a whisper

Hey, I've got the light
You've got the shade
But do what you like
I'm not afraid
I got bolder

I've got the winning ways
But you've got the Monkey Shoulder
Yeah, yeah, yeah, yeah,
The Monkey Shoulder

There's me and there's you
One and one's two
Here's what we'll do
I'll make it up to you
And we'll do a little shaking
Till my arms are aching
With all the mixing and making

The burn and the ice
The sweet and the tang
The dark and the nice
Just like Tristan
And Isolde

She had a winking eye
And he got the Monkey Shoulder
Yeah, yeah, yeah, yeah
The Monkey Shoulder

I liked the style of Monkey Shoulder when it first appeared courtesy of William Grant & Sons. I liked the quirky name (which had apparently been used to describe a medical condition that malt men suffered from, as a result of shovelling malt for hours on end); I liked the packaging, especially the three monkeys embossed on the bottle (not the see-no, hear-no, speak-no monkeys, which in Scotland would probably be four anyway, but three monkeys on each other's back); and I liked the website, despite the fact that it was clearly aimed at a younger age group than the one I got caught up in. On that website I saw a number of recipes for interesting cocktails, some of them monkey twists on older drinks — Monkey Manhattan, Monkey Mule, Monkey Mojito, etc, etc. So that got me thinking about a conference of mixologists, a young man and a young woman attracted to each other — flirting, teasing and fighting over the Monkey Shoulder. A good relationship is like a well-made cocktail after all — the whole is greater than the sum of the parts.

Heaven Hill

SONG • RECORDED ON ONE FOR THE ROAD • CDTRAX313

There's a woman who lives on Heaven Hill
Lord! She is my kind of girl
She keeps me free from the winter chill
Out on the porch at night

She intoxicates me by degrees
And mostly has me on my knees
Doing the things that she knows will please
Me – up on Heaven Hill

We drank whiskey from an old stone jar
We made love in a Mustang car
We lay back and we watched the stars
High on Heaven Hill

It's hard to come down from Heaven Hill
I know I have to but I don't have the will
When we're together, oh it's such a thrill
She takes my breath away

She's got honey she's got spice
She's pepper hot and she's cold as ice
She's got what it takes to entice
Me – up on Heaven Hill

We drank whiskey from an old stone jar...

Oh the moon shines down on Heaven Hill
I do believe it always will
In my mind I can see her still
Reaching a hand out to me

She made me feel I was in space
Swinging her dark hair over my face
And all the stars in the Universe chased
Me – high over Heaven Hill

We drank whiskey from an old stone jar
We made love in a Mustang car
We lay back and we travelled to the stars
High on Heaven Hill
We got high on Heaven Hill
High on Heaven Hill

The first Bourbon I had from the Scotch Malt Whisky Society was a 20 year old Heaven Hill. Now and then I would pour a large glass of this, over ice, and settle down late at night to watch a DVD of the Dixie Chicks in concert. I wrote the song when all I had to go on was the name of the distillery – so it is pure fantasy; moreover, the song deliberately mixes up the woman and the whiskey – which one did I love more?

Johnnie and Me

SONG • RECORDED ON WHISKY AND DEATH • FW001CD

There's a country in my memory
I still visit now and then
A place of innocence and harmony
Before the shadows cast by men
Sometimes it seems
That there's only one guy
On whom you really can depend
And I say ooh ooh
Ooh ooh
I'm taking Johnnie Walker home with me tonight

Looking back as far as I can see
It's a sad rear mirror view
If my life has been a tapestry
It's all been done in black and blue
And I beat myself up
With all those 'might have beens'
But I don't know what else to do
So I sing ooh ooh
Ooh ooh
I'm taking Johnnie Walker home with me tonight

When I'm feeling small
I can rely on him to call
Even in the middle of the night
Johnnie comes round
And he says 'Ooh Baby
Everything will be alright
Just hold me tight'

I'm not looking for no sympathy
Don't want to sound like Patsy Cline
Yes I wish I'd done things differently
But at least the choices were all mine
Cos if you don't take chances
Then your dreams can't fly
They'll only wither on the vine
So I say ooh ooh
Ooh ooh
I'm taking Johnnie Walker home with me tonight

All you other guys
Just get over it and dry your eyes
Maybe some day your turn will come
But not tonight!
Ooh ooh ooh ooh
Tonight's gonna be
Just Johnnie and me

Sometimes love is like a lottery
Sometimes a roller coaster ride
Broken dreams and broken crockery
A broken heart you try to hide
I lost my way, sometimes
I even lost hope
But I never lost my pride
So I'm singing ooh ooh
Ooh ooh
I'm taking Johnnie, he's my honey
He's always worth the money
I'm taking Johnnie Walker home with me tonight

At a Keepers of the Quaich event a few years ago at Gleneagles Hotel, I sat next to Paul Walsh, CEO of Diageo at that time. He asked me why I had not written any songs about Diageo brands. That set me thinking and this came out — it's my attempt to write a country song — but from a woman's point of view.

The Wee Cooper o' Fife

SONG • TUNE – THE WEE COOPER O' FIFE

There was a wee cooper who lived in Fife
Butts and barrels and hoggies too
He worked at Cameron Brig a' his life
Shavin' a stave and a hoop for the cooper
And dechar rechar, mak it anew

He invented a centrifugal machine
Butts and barrels and hoggies too
To spin the barrels an' sook them clean
Shavin' a stave and a hoop for the cooper
And dechar rechar, mak it anew

The dregs o' the whisky would hit the slide
Butts and barrels and hoggies too
Till not a drappie was left inside
Shavin' a stave and a hoop for the cooper
And dechar rechar, mak it anew

This cooper got wed to a gentle wife
Butts and barrels and hoggies too
But soon he became the scourge of her life
Shavin' a stave and a hoop for the cooper
And dechar rechar, mak it anew

For she never saw him sober at hame
Butts and barrels and hoggies too
The centrifugal machine was to blame
Shavin' a stave and a hoop for the cooper
And dechar rechar, mak it anew

One night when the cooper had been on the skyte
Butts and barrels and hoggies too
She trussed him up in an old port pipe
Shavin' a stave and a hoop for the cooper
And dechar rechar, mak it anew

An old port pipe missing three staves
Butts and barrels and hoggies too
Fitted her husband as snug as the grave
Shavin' a stave and a hoop for the cooper
And dechar rechar, mak it anew

All that stuck out was his head and his feet
Butts and barrels and hoggies too
And these wi' a stave she proceeded to beat
Shavin' a stave and a hoop for the cooper
And dechar rechar, mak it anew

The cooper did roar the cooper did greet
Butts and barrels and hoggies too
But she rolled the poor devil along the street
Shavin' a stave and a hoop for the cooper
And dechar rechar, mak it anew

Now he's back at his work in the coopering shop
Butts and barrels and hoggies too
But never mair will he touch a drop
Shavin' a stave and a hoop for the cooper
And dechar rechar, mak it anew

The old song, The Wee Cooper o' Fife, is not sung very much these days, probably because it is about a man who beats his wife because she won't do the housework. I thought it a shame that the only song we have about a cooper (apart from The Cooper o' Cuddy, a rather crude one by Robert Burns) was not being sung, so I re-wrote it to make it less offensive, and now in my version, it is the woman who beats up the man — for being frequently drunk, something that may well have been an issue for a cooper.

Cameronbridge (Cameron Brig to the locals) is the biggest distillery in Scotland, producing grain whisky, Gordon's gin and Smirnoff vodka.

The nonsense refrain from the original (nickety nackety noo noo noo etc) has been replaced with coopering terms — 'dechar rechar' is a process for rejuvenating tired casks so that they might better influence the whisky. The char on the inside of the cask is scraped away and the wood charred once more, caramelising the natural sugars in the oak.

Ugly Betty

SONG • RECORDED ON WHISKY AND DEATH • FW001CD

I love my Ugly Betty
OK she's rough and ready
But what she gives me in the end
May not be nutritious
But it's suspiciously delicious
And she will always be my friend

When I dance with Ugly Betty
It always feels so right
Together we glide
Side by side
Beneath the pale moonlight

Whatever mood I'm in
I'm in the mood for gin
I hear those violins
And I am gone

My love for Ugly Betty
Gets me giddy and unsteady
My sense of balance gets confused
I stagger and I stumble
I mumble and I fumble
My feet get tripped up by my shoes

But when I kiss my Ugly Betty
It's always sexy and slow
She tingles my lip
And the little tender tip
Of my tongue gets a tickly glow

Whatever mood I'm in
I'm in the mood for gin
I hear those violins
And I am gone

When I'm with Ugly Betty
My dreams fall like confetti
Happy thoughts raining down on me
My cup is flowing over
I'm rolling in the clover
Gee I love my G and T

And when I talk to Ugly Betty
She doesn't have a lot to say
But between me and you
I can talk enough for two
And Betty smiles to tell me that's OK

Whatever mood I'm in
I'm in the mood for gin
It surely is no sin
If it dribbles down my chin
And I've got this crazy grin
Like I'm in a loony bin
Please call my next of kin
Cos I am gone
Solid gone

OK — this is a gin song — so what's it doing in a whisky book? The gin they make at Bruichladdich Distillery is called The Botanist and the two things that make it interesting are — firstly, that it contains 22 plant species that are foraged on Islay. Secondly, it is re-distilled with those plants and other aromatics in a Lomond still that came from Dumbarton distillery. Lomond stills were versatile bits of equipment, but never that good to look at. The staff at Bruichladdich nicknamed this one Ugly Betty and one year when I was looking for a subject for a new Bruichladdich song, this is what I came up with.

After swimming in the sea on Islay and walking over the beach with that entire sensation of the Hebridean tingle — tasting the salt, smelling the floral aromas of the machair and feeling the sun on your goose-pimpled skin, my wife invented a Hebridean Tingle cocktail — ice, salt-rimmed glass, Botanist gin, tonic, lime and Innocent mango and passion-fruit smoothie from the Bowmore Co-op — fabulous! — nearly as good as a decent dram. That isn't to say there is any connection between my wife and a song called Ugly Betty — so don't get any ideas.

Whisky Widow

SONG • TUNE – THE TINKER'S WEDDING

So Charlie's half a century young
This spring chicken's spring is sprung
And I would like to see him hung
In Demarco's Gallery-o

A dram or two or three a day
Four or five he's well away
He has to drink to earn his pay
It's a hard life being Charlie-o

At breakfast, brunch or business lunch
Or every book that gets a launch
As long as there's ladles o' whisky
      punch
He's in the hurly-burly-o.

We hae three sons – three laddies braw
They get bedtime stories from their
      paw
But he reads himsel' tae sleep an' a'
Snorin' like a Harley-o.

A dram or two or three a day
Four or five he's well away
He has to drink to earn his pay
It's a hard life being Charlie-o

He says he only taks a gill
Whenever he is feeling ill
It's better than a Prozac pill
If you're feeling peelie-wallie-o

For he often wakens in a dwam
Rolling eyes and trembling palms
Until he reaches for a dram
That fixes him entirely-o

A dram or two or three a day
Four or five he's well away
He has to drink to earn his pay
It's a hard life being Charlie-o

He swans aboot the art-lit scene
And exotic places he has been
He even went to visit the Queen
Doon at Buckie Paly-o

Says she 'Oh, Charlie, just the man
Come away ben and hae a dram'
Says he 'Well thank you kindly Ma'am
Open a bloody barrel-o'

A dram or two or three a day
Four or five he's well away
He has to drink to earn his pay
It's a hard life being Charlie-o

When he's lookin' flash in his tartan sash
He cuts a rather dapper dash
But what came first – man or moustache?
I'll tell you fair and squarely-o

There's a family photie in a frame
O' Charlie as a pre-school wean
On his moustache a chocolate stain
In his hand the juice o' the barley-o

A dram or two or three a day
Four or five he's well away
He has to drink to earn his pay
It's a hard life being Charlie-o

His lip is thick wi' bristly hair
Kissin' him maks your ain lip sair
He once kissed Hercules the bear
He thought it was a girlie-o.

He's in a club it's called the Spec
Its members are a' physical wrecks
From whacking whisky owre their necks
And acting quite bizarrely-o

A dram or two or three a day
Four or five he's well away
He has to drink to earn his pay
It's a hard life being Charlie-o

He's often seen to take a sip
From a flask he wears upon his hip
But I got him a permanent whisky-drip
To hasten his grand finale-o

And from the roof-tops I will yell
A whisky widow's life is hell
It'd drive ye tae the drink yersel
Puttin' up wi' Charlie-o

A dram or two or three a day
Four or five he's well away
He has to drink to earn his pay
It's a hard life being married to Charlie-o

When my friend and mentor, Charlie MacLean became 50, his wife asked me to write a wee song for the party. I think she maybe wanted a glowing panegyric for Charlie – but she got this instead.

IX

Whisky in its Place

A region, a distillery, a bar, a warehouse, a boat
— whisky draws pilgrims to all those places.

The Speyside Whisky Song
Reaching Home
Bruichladdich
Whisky Cathedral
Islay Roads
The Hills of Ardnahoe
Jasper 'Jack' D.
The Smallest Whisky Bar
The *Sentosa* Sails Away

The Speyside Whisky Song

SONG • TUNE – THE ROAD TO THE ISLES

By Benromach and Balmenach and Benriach I will go
For the Whisky River's calling me away
By Tormore and Tamnavoulin, by Aultmore and Tomintoul
For a spiritual sprauchle by the Spey

By Macallan and Glendullan and Glenallachie we'll go
Distilleries unfolding by the score
By Kininvie and Craigellachie, Mortlach and Auchroisk
Pittyvaich and Miltonduff and Mannochmore

There's a wee dram waiting at the end of every mile
From Dufftown all the way to Dallas Dhu
And a wee sensation that will surely make you smile
At Knockando, Caperdonich and Cardhu.

From Glenrothes to Gentauchers, from Glenfarclas to Glenspey
From Glen Moray to Glen Elgin and Glen Grant
From Glenfiddich to Glenlossie, from Glenlivet to Glen Keith
I'm a whisky-sipping Speyside sycophant

There's Braeval and there's Benrinnes, Linkwood and Cragganmore
Then there's Speyburn and Strathisla and Strathmill
There's Inchgower, Aberlour, Longmorn and Tamdhu
And the only problem's picking up the bill

And the Spey runs sweetly from the mountains to the sea
Through scenery so stunning and sublime
There are angels everywhere, soaking up their share
Aye and that's OK as long as I get mine

For the heid or for the body, taken neat or in a toddy
As a medicine it canny be surpassed
If you're fightin' aff a lurgie, you can gargle wi' Glenburgie
If you're feeling rather blue then try a double o' Dailuaine
If you're miserable and flu-ish hae a drappie o' Drumguish
And for ony kind o' pain scoop a shot o' Allt a Bhainne
And Balvenie is Viagra in a glass

A few years ago I wrote a book about the distilleries of Speyside (The Whisky River). *While researching the book by visiting distilleries and tasting their wares (aye, it's a hard job, but someone has to do it!) I thought about writing a song to see how many of the distillery names I could get in. In the end, I managed all 53 — some are missing here because the rhymes were a bit naughty so I didn't want to record them on the CD. The missing names were Imperial, Coleburn and Convalmore — oh, and now Roseisle — they go in the last section of the song, so you can maybe work out what the ailments were that rhymed with the names.*

To use the tune of The Road to the Isles when writing about Speyside was ironic and even a wee bit cheeky — but it works.

Reaching Home

SONG • RECORDED ON ONE FOR THE ROAD • CDTRAX313

The sun is warm, the air is clear and still
Soon we'll be standing on the pier
They chased the Devil from the church on the hill
And they offer you angels' tears
I never knew the name
Of the angel who flew too close to the flame
And maybe, maybe,
Maybe I never will

The sun is climbing high overhead
The distance fading from the view
A wisp of smoke is a homespun thread
Through silver and gold and blue
It comes as no surprise
That all these years under foreign skies
Has made me, made me,
Made me lose the thread

You can come in the night
Like a silkie from the sea
Eyes quick and bright
Full of destiny
Or like a broken king
In the hour before the dawn
Hoping to find your Avalon
Sun on the water makes you feel you can fly
Smoke on the water makes you cry
Smoke on the water makes you cry

Dusk is here and far in the west
Soon the fire will be gone
Reaching home is the hardest test
With the darkest night coming on
The ship of legend turns
And the mariner knows the sweetness that burns
And says he, says he,
Says he'll return at dawn

You can come in the night...

As part of the Feis Ile I once did a tasting and concert in No 1 Vault at Bowmore. For the event I researched lots of Islay stories, some of which I have made into poems and some of which I re-told in my book Whisky Legends of Islay. *This is the only song I have written about Bowmore and it tries to pick up the theme of those legends and tales. Reaching Home was one of their website strap-lines at that time and they had various expressions in bottles and tins that told the tales of the Sea Dragon, The Maid of Islay etc. I incorporated some of their lovely, evocative whisky names into the song — Dawn, Dusk, Legend, Mariner and Darkest, though most of those names are no longer in use. The song also reflects the idea of people returning to the island after long exile — few places have a more magnetic draw than Islay on those islanders who left for work, education, adventure or whatever — could it be something to do with the whisky?*

Bruichladdich

SONG • RECORDED ON THE WATER OF LIFE • CDTRAX246

One day as I was walking by the shores of Loch Indaal
I met a man with sadness in his eye
His story was as haunted as the lonely sea-bird's call
And he told me of the day he turned and walked away
As he watched the fire at Bruichladdich die

He told me of a place that once would never sleep
With hiss of steam and clang and furnace roar
And how that sleeping beauty lies trapped in slumber deep
With moonbeams full of dust and gates in chains of rust
And ghosts that wander the Bruichladdich floor

The moon smiles kindly on the western seas
Perfume tumbles on the midnight breeze
Standing on the island of distilleries
You can almost see the coast of heaven

Here I stand again after years have gone by
With a Bruichladdich in my hands once more
It reminds me of the magic of a moonlit sky
The way it catches light and smells of summer nights
And the sea that touches the Bruichladdich shore

The moon smiles kindly on the western seas...

So I'll drink to the men who saw a tiny spark
And thought that they could turn it to a flame
The men who chased a dream and dragged it from the dark
To see the light of day and fought to find a way
To bring new meaning to the Bruichladdich name

The moon smiles kindly on the western seas...

This was the first song about Bruichladdich that I wrote. It was partly a celebration of the re-opening of a closed distillery, but it was also a personal tribute to Jim McEwan, who left his job of 38 years at Bowmore to help revive Bruichladdich. It was Martine Nouet who put the idea into my head and the first time Jim heard the song was at Martine's whisky festival in Paris — at a dinner on board a restaurant boat moored on the River Seine.

Whisky Cathedral

SONG • RECORDED ON WHISKY AND DEATH • FW001CD

I dream of a place on the Rinns of Islay
A place where I'm always longing to be
A place where the fluttering wings of angels
Are constantly cooling and comforting me

There's wood from the Ozark oaks of Missouri
There's wood from the fabled forests of France
And every cask contains golden treasure –
That's why the angels all play harps and dance

In the warehouse at Bruichladdich
I drink therefore I am
A whisky cathedral
Where angels are singing
In praise of glorious drams

The names that I see are the lines of a litany
Margaux, Petrus, Latour and Lafitte
Gonzalez Byass, Jim Beam and Jack Daniels
Our spirits are raised and our joy is complete.

Some people say that the whisky is sinful
And may lead you down into the abyss
But whisky can light up the road to salvation
A heavenly dram is a moment of bliss

In the warehouse...

And what better place than the Rinns of Islay
To fondly recall my whisky career
So many moments and so many blessings
And most of the best ones have all happened here

In the warehouse at Bruichladdich
I drink therefore I am
A whisky cathedral
Where angels are singing
In praise of glorious drams
In praise, praise, in praise, in praise of glorious drams

It is hard to over-emphasise the importance of the cask in determining the final character of whisky. Wood management policies can make the difference between an ordinary distillery and a great one. Few distilleries take this aspect more seriously than Bruichladdich and when you stand in their warehouse and see the names on the casks — all the bourbon, sherry, port, red wine and sweet white wine cask provenance — it is amazing, instructive and reassuring.

To have the opportunity to taste whisky straight from the cask in the warehouse where it sleeps is one of the best experiences one can have. No wonder the angels hang out there.

Islay Roads

SONG • TUNE – TAKE ME HOME COUNTRY ROADS (JOHN DENVER)

Almost Heaven, Bruichladdich
A whisky fountain, everybody's happy
Life is good there, in that whisky vault
Keep your misty moonshine – we want single malt!

Islay roads, take me there
To the place I love best
Bruichladdich
Whisky Mamma
Close to Heaven
In the west.

Catch the ferry, cross the water
End your journey with a glass of nectar
Watch the sunset colouring the sky
Back again on Islay, teardrop in my eye

Islay roads, take me there
To the place I love best
Bruichladdich
Whisky Mamma
Close to Heaven
In the west.

Clouds roll by and the wind moves the barley
Salt on the air from the fine ocean spray
And standing with my dram I get the feeling
That I could come here every day, every day

Islay roads, take me there
To the place I love best
Bruichladdich
Whisky Mamma
Close to Heaven
In the west.

Islay roads, take me there
To the place I love best
Bruichladdich
Whisky Mamma
Close to Heaven
In the west.

'The Coast of Heaven'
Is in the west.

> *Travelling through Germany by train with Jim McEwan a couple of years ago, he told me that the theme of the next Bruichladdich Open Day was going to be 'Country and Western' — we started to toss ideas around for a song that might suit the occasion — and this was the result.*

The Hills of Ardnahoe

SONG • TUNE – THE HILLS OF ILE AU HAUT (GORD'ON BOK)

Oh a wise man once declared
That life is a winding road
And the journey's always harder
When you carry a heavy load

Come let us go
On that winding road together
We'll spend a peaceful day
By the hills of Ardnahoe

When the sun is to the Westward
And the stormy clouds have passed
You can catch that golden sunset
And its warmth inside a glass

Come let us go…

When the toast is absent friends
And a tear is in your eye
Let the spirit lift your spirit
Into a bright blue sky

Come let us go…

When the rain is driving sideways
And you're tired of the ice and snow
Just pour a dram of nectar
And dream of Ardnahoe

Come let us go…

With a bottle in your knapsack
And singing as you go
That winding road goes westward
And leads to Ardnahoe

Come let us go…

Ardnahoe is the latest distillery project on Islay. It is the dream project of the Hunter Laing team and is situated in a beautiful spot on the road to Bunnahbhain, looking over the Sound of Islay to the Paps of Jura. Now we have yet another reason to head west and visit the magical Isle of Islay.

Jasper (Jack) D.

SONG • RECORDED ON WHISKY AND DEATH • FW001CD

I took a little trip to Lynchburg, Moore County, Tennessee
I wanted to visit the spiritual home of good old Jasper (Jack) D.
But when I got to Lynchburg I couldn't get a drop to try
The man in the place laughed in my face – 'Sorry, Lynchburg's dry'.

Dry as a bone, dry as a stone
Dry as fake tears down the telephone
Dry as tumbleweed rolling in the dust
Dry as a flame on a flake of rust
There's nowhere as dry as the spiritual home
Of good old Jasper (Jack) D.

I must have looked kind of bewildered 'cos the man began to explain
He said 'Lynchburg's dry as a Scotchman's purse, no matter how much it rains.
If you ask for a drink in Lynchburg you're always gonna be refused
Since nineteen-o-nine this town of mine is a place where you can't buy booze'.

Dry as a well when the oil is gone
Dry as toast with no butter on
Dry as a tick in a tiger's coat
Dry – so dry it sticks in my throat
There's nowhere as dry as the spiritual home
Of good old Jasper (Jack) D.

Jack Daniel wouldn't like it
It would make him cry
The home of Tennessee Sour Mash
Is dry as a shovel-full of cigar ash
The last place you can make a splash
Is here – 'cos Lynchburg's dry.

'You can hunt like Davy Crockett, you can lie like Monica's Bill
You can wheedle and plead till your eyeballs bleed but you can't get a quarter gill
The angels here get plenty — poor sinners we get none
So don't think twice, take my advice — and head for Kentucky, Son!'

Dry as your mouth after you're sick
Dry as an oven for baking a brick
Dry as a gulch where warthogs play
Or a sinner's tongue on Judgement Day
There's nowhere as dry as the spiritual home
Of good old Jasper (Jack) D.

I thought it was funny that the biggest distillery in the US and its best known whiskey export is made in a place where it is not possible to buy a drink. Surely that was reason enough to compose a song. Jasper Daniel (Jack was his nickname) died in 1911 from blood poisoning — the story goes that he injured his toe after kicking his safe because he had forgotten the combination. This was shortly after Moore County went dry — maybe that was what made him angry! Prohibition ended in 1933, but it was not repealed in Tennessee. Individual counties can opt by referendum to bring back booze, but Moore County never has, in spite of the fact (or maybe because of the fact) that whiskey making is its main industry and primary source of wealth. Davy Crockett was one of Tennessee's famous sons.

The Smallest Whisky Bar

SONG • RECORDED ON WHISKY FOR BREAKFAST • CDTRAX361

I will follow my star
To the smallest whisky bar on earth
And we will see
What we might see over there
In Santa Maria
In Val Mustair

Would you like to come too?
I am sure that you will find
Just like me
Everything will feel alright
In Santa Maria
Where it's warm at night

I can't resist the call
Over mountains and miles
I could be there by nightfall
In Santa Maria

We can go in my car
And though it's far to drive
At journey's end
We'll find new friends I know
Santa Maria
Is the place to go

There are no clichés
It's the funkiest place I know
It may be small
But within these walls you'll find
In Santa Maria
Some peace of mind

I can't resist the call…

In that tiny bar
Gunter and Macbutton serve
And Detlef too
With passion true and rare
In Santa Maria
Good spirits there

I can't resist the call…

My friend, Gunter Sommer, has the smallest whisky bar on Earth (accredited as such by the Guinness Book of Records) in Santa Maria in Val Mustair, Switzerland. This place is a hoot! It is cosy and friendly and has a really interesting selection of whiskies — only whiskies — no beer, wine or other spirits. Given that it is only about 8.5 square metres, you can understand that. Gunter also has a whisky museum underneath the bar and his own (High Glen) distillery up the road. He is passionate about whisky and always has lots of stories and opinions. I have done the occasional gig there, but we have to limit the numbers to about 10!

Santa Maria is a beautiful village, very close to the Italian border. To get there from anywhere else in Switzerland, you have to go over the Ofen Pass; high mountains, hairpin bends, etc. — but it really is worth it!

The *Sentosa* Sails Away

SONG • RECORDED ON WHISKY AND DEATH • FW001CD

The Sentosa sails away…
And the sun is going down
It's been another working day
Crazy in its way
But now the sun is going down

The city noise is left behind
And the water is so calm
I've got nothing on my mind
In fact I'm feeling fine
I'm happy where I am

We've got glasses in our hands
And a smile on every face
It's not hard to understand
That anyone could find
A taste of heaven in this place

The Sentosa sails away…

Sorrow's never far away
And we wonder where it all might end
But just for today
We've got good whisky and good friends.

Captain Kurt is in command
His reputation is well known
With strong coffee in his hand
For he never takes a dram
He will bring us safely home

The city noise is left behind
And the water is so calm
I've got nothing on my mind
In fact I'm feeling fine
I am happy where I am

The Sentosa sails away...
The Sentosa sails away...

One of my regular gigs in Switzerland was aboard the Sentosa – sailing out of Zurich, we would head up the lake almost as far as Horgen where the ferry runs across. Kurt and Theres were very genial hosts and the whiskies would be provided either by Yvonne Zürcher or Daniel Graf (who would also welcome people by playing his bagpipes on the quay). This lovely, compact boat would accommodate about 25 people and the atmosphere was always really special and friendly. People enjoyed it so much they would always try to come back again and again – so it became a kind of small but regular community of whisky and music lovers.

We would introduce and serve whiskies, along with some interesting finger food and some entertainment from me. When we got to the middle of Lake Zurich, Kurt would cut the engines and I would sing a couple of more thoughtful or lyrical songs as we bobbed in the darkness. Kurt and Therese sold the Sentosa however and those glorious evenings watching the sun go down with good friends and fine whiskies are only a memory now – but celebrated in this song.

X

Nothing Succeeds Like Excess

You couldn't have a collection of whisky songs and poems without at least a few that involve drinking LARGE amounts!

Oh Lord
Usquebaugh Baul
We can't let Al Qaeda get their Hands on This
Loons is Loons
Shackleton's Hut
The Missionary
Snuffed Out

Oh Lord

SONG • TUNE – MERCEDES BENZ (JANIS JOPLIN)

Oh Lord, won't you buy me a Mercedes-Benz
A great big stretch-limo – with room for all my friends
And a bar in the back, full of good malts and blends
Oh Lord, won't you buy me a Mercedes-Benz

Lord, won't you buy me a night on the town
My friends are all wusses – they always let me down
So prove that you love me and buy the next round
Oh Lord, won't you buy me a night on the town.

Lord, won't you buy me a bottle of Black Bowmore
Just you and me Lord, we'll double lock the door
The Devil will be jealous, but him we can ignore
Oh Lord, won't you buy me a bottle of Black Bowmore.

Lord, won't you buy me my own whisky cask
You say you can do anything – I'm taking you to task
A barrel or a hoggie – it's the last thing I'll ask
Oh Lord, won't you buy me my own whisky cask.

Lord, why don't you buy me a whole distillery
My liver might suffer but my soul will be set free
And I'll be in Heaven – if you make it all tax free!
Oh Lord, won't you buy me a whole distillery.

This is a whisky prayer, in which each verse represents a steady increase in the level of demand, until it reaches the almost unobtainable — I think each time I had a dram the horizons of possibility grew. It's just as well I stopped at five! I think Janis Joplin would have understood where I was coming from.

Usquebaugh Baul

SONG • RECORDED ON ONE FOR THE ROAD • CDTRAX313

Usquebaugh Baul, Usquebaugh Baul
High intensity alcohol
Exceedingly risky, it's perilous whisky
One sip and you'll stumble and fall

Usquebaugh Baul is four times distilled
Some say it cures and some say it kills
Take my advice and make out a will
Before you drink Usquebaugh Baul

Take one sip but don't take a second
It packs more punch than ever you reckoned
You'll spin in the wind like the Corryvrekkan
With dangerous Usquebaugh Baul

Usquebaugh Baul, Usquebaugh Baul...

The island of Islay has numerous wrecks
Mostly from flinging it over their necks
And now here's a dram that's better than sex
Four times Usquebaugh Baul

This is the stuff to put out your lights
It kicks, it bites; it's like kryptonite
You can lie on the floor but you have to hold tight
For you're spinning with Usquebaugh Baul

Usquebaugh Baul, Usquebaugh Baul...

And you'll be on the losing side
Too late to run, no place to hide
You've passed the point where you know what you're doing
Facing the end – the final ruin – cursing poor Jim McEwan
'cos you're on the losing side – you're on the losing side

One spoonful your heart's beating fast
Two spoonfuls you're feeling quite gassed
Three spoonfuls you've breathed your last
You're in the past – Oh, What a blast – Usquebaugh Baul

Usquebaugh Baul, Usquebaugh Baul
High Intensity, 17th Century,
Savage ferocity, super velocity
Wonderful Usquebaugh Baul!

Four times distilled whisky was described in a book by Martin Martin A Description of the Western Islands of Scotland *as Usquebaugh Baul – a potent spirit 'which at first taste affects all the Members of the Body: two spoonfuls of this last Liquor is a sufficient Dose; and if any Man exceed this, it would presently stop his Breath, and endanger his Life'. Of course Mark Reynier and Jim McEwan at Bruichladdich thought it would be a good idea to make some. Usquebaugh Baul is gaelic for perilous whisky.*

I was invited to attend on the first occasion it was produced – along with some people from the TV and newspapers. At the end of an interesting few hours, we were all given souvenir bottles of new make spirit with special labels – Bruichladdich Usquebaugh Baul at 89.9%ABV – signed by managing director Mark Reynier. All the others had them taken away at the airport because anything over 70%ABV is classified as a hazardous substance. Being a penniless songwriter, I was on the ferry and so I am probably the only person in the world with this special bottle.

You can still buy the four times distilled whisky from Bruichladdich but it is now called X4 and it is definitely not sold at 89.9%ABV. At full strength it has been used to power a Radical racing car, famously by Oz Clarke and James May on their TV series Oz and James Drink to Britain.

We Can't let Al Qaeda get their Hands on This

SONG • RECORDED ON ONE FOR THE ROAD • CDTRAX313

There's a secret installation on the western seas
Cunningly disguised among the Hebrides
It might seem innocent to those who are naive
But this could bring a super power to its knees.

Now I am a US Internet spy
And I've seen what they're up to with my own eyes
They say it's only whisky but I'm tellin' you,
They tested it on the local folk and I've seen what it can do.

So be careful how you're steppin'
Round this deadly lethal weapon
And tell all the patriots it's time to enlist
We've got to take some action
'Gainst this weapon of mass distraction
Oh we can't let Al Qaeda get their hands on this.

The scary thing is it's made from a kind of grass
With biological action to give it critical mass
And if they get it up to 90 ABV
It's going to be an awesome WMD

I got me a sample and sent it to the lab
The lab report came back saying 'Man this stuff's not bad!'
So I am defecting – 'cos one thing's clear
I'd rather die from this stuff than from American beer!

So be careful how you're steppin'...

This is based on a true story – the American Government was spying on Bruichladdich through the web-cams because their traditional distilling equipment could, apparently, be used for the manufacture of chemical weapons. Bruichladdich wanted to put my song on their website but they were wary of upsetting the Americans as that is a sizeable market – so I agreed to change the last two lines to:

So telephone the President 'cos one thing is clear
It's the Tartan Army America should fear.

However, some time later, they decided to be brave and put the original version up. It didn't seem to damage their sales in the US.

Loons is Loons

SONG • RECORDED ON WHISKY FOR BREAKFAST • CDTRAX361

'Loons is loons the warld roond
But Rothes loons is buggers'
The whisky pipe got drilled one night
And the hale toon gathered roond
The pipe got drilled, and the pots got filled,
And they a' got fu' thegither

Major Grant was a decent soul
And the toonfolk loved him well
So why they did this terrible thing
Not one of them could tell
But whisky flowing through a pipe
Suspended in mid-air
Was just a touch temptation
More than some of them could bear

Loons is loons…

Some men dream of a bottle of drams
Some men dream of a still
But what could please a body more
Than an auger and a drill
You'd never need to do any work
And neither buy nor sell
But just enjoy the trickle and flow
Of your very own 'secret well'

Loons is loons…

But the Rothes loons upset the Lord
Wi' their wicked, sinful deeds
An' retribution came to them a'
In the form of achin' heids
So they made a contract wi' the Lord
To leave the pipe on Sunday
For a double dose the night before
Would see them through till Monday

'Loons is loons the world roond
But Rothes loons is buggers'
The whisky pipe got drilled one night
And the hale toon gathered roond
The pipe got drilled, and the pots got filled,
And they a' got fu'
Roarin' fu'
The air was blue
What a hulabaloo
Big galoots
As pissed as newts
Suckin' it oot o'dirty cloots;
They a' got fu' thegither

The story of the famous 'whisky pipe' in downtown Rothes is this; Glen Grant was the first distillery to be built in Rothes (1840) and in time it became very successful (perhaps due to its claim that the purifiers on the stills made a healthier whisky). The route to expansion they chose was to build Glen Grant No 2 distillery on the other side of the main road. The stills, the water, the process was exactly the same as in Glen Grant No 1. Unfortunately, the Customs and Excise insisted that all Glen Grant should be bottled at the original distillery, so the company built a pipe across the road, carrying the new make from the new distillery to the old. The pipe was high enough to allow horses and carts etc to travel along the road underneath.

Enterprising young men of Rothes (and eventually from other towns) discovered the possibility of drilling holes in the pipe, capturing the spirit and stopping the holes with wax. This free bar continued for some time, the owners suspecting nothing, until one particularly hot summer, the sun melted the wax – it was raining booze and something had to be done.

'Loons is loons the world roond, but Rothes loons is buggers' was a phrase given to me by Richard Forsyth, owner of the Rothes-based coppersmiths. He attributed it to Biawa Makalaga, a black man who lived in Rothes until he died aged 85, in 1972. He had been brought there as a boy of 6 from Matabeleland by Major Grant. He was a well-known character in the town and some of his expressions have slipped into the folk memory.

Shackleton's Hut

SONG • RECORDED ON WHISKY AND DEATH • FW001CD

I'm gonna fly across to Jamaica
Then I'll swim to the Yucatan
I'll get to Venezuela
Any way I can
I'll cycle down the Andes
Right to the very tip
At Tierra del Fuego
I'll climb aboard a ship

Across the Weddell Sea
That ship will carry me
Gonna cleanse my soul
At the Southern Pole

My life has lost its meaning
I think I'm in a rut
It's time for some spring cleaning
And a month or two in Shackleton's hut

I won't take anything with me
Except for my teddy bear
I guess it could get lonely
Depends how long I'm there
I won't miss the television
It's a poison in my brain
A drop of Shackleton's whisky
Will help to keep me sane

Underneath the floor
There's sixty bottles or more
Gonna dig a little hole
At the Southern Pole

My life has lost its meaning...

Now Ernest was a good guy
Respected by all his men
He took them to the world's edge
And brought them back again
He embraced adventure
Every single day
And he knew the power of whisky
To keep the cold at bay

Mr Shackleton could be
A good role model for me
I'm gonna rock and roll
At the Southern Pole

My life has lost its meaning...

Now I've reached Antarctica
I landed with the tide
But a friendly penguin told me
The hut's on the other side
I guess I'd better start walking
It'll help to keep me warm
A little bit of exercise
Never did me any harm

So Pingo come with me
I could use some company
We'll waddle and we'll stroll
To the Southern Pole

My life has lost its meaning...

After hearing the story of how a substantial stash of whisky was discovered encased in ice, under the floor of Shackleton's Hut at Cape Royds in Antarctica, and more importantly, that it had been found to be in good condition for drinking — and then put back where it was! — I started to fantasise about making a trip there.

It turns out that one of the sponsors of the Shackleton expedition of 1909 was Mackinlay's Whisky, supplying 25 cases at 47.3% abv, to help it withstand the cold. The crew drank most of it, to help them withstand the cold — but it was jolly decent of them to leave some for me.

The Missionary

SONG • TUNE – MRS McGRATH

Well a missionary Jock near Victoria Falls
One day got captured by the cannibals
They tied him up and they put him in a pot
They lit up a fire and it grew quite hot.

Wi' my toor-i-a foldi-riddle-da
Toor-i-oor-i-oor-i-a
Wi' my toor-i-a foldi-riddle-da
Toor-i-oor-i-oor-i-a

The missionary cried to the chief of the tribe
'Are you open to persuasion or perhaps to a bribe?
Is there nae mercy, nae court of appeal?
Cos I don't want to end up as an evening meal.'

Wi' my toor-i-a foldi-riddle-da...

The chief of the cannibals scratched his head
And he laughed at the missionary as he said
'Well you wouldnae make much of an evening meal
So I'll let you have a go at the trial by ordeal.'

Wi' my toor-i-a foldi-riddle-da...

Now the first thing you have to do is risky
It's to knock back a gallon of oor African whisky
Then you run to that cave on the mountainside
Where a terrible sabre-toothed tiger bides.

Wi' my toor-i-a foldi-riddle-da...

And that sabre-toothed tiger has got two big teeth –
And you have to pull them out and bring them back to the chief
Then you have to sleep with the chief's first bride
And she has never been satisfied!

Wi' my toor-i-a foldi-riddle-da...

Well the missionary knocked back the African whisky
First he got happy and then he got frisky
And he staggered up the hill feeling flushed and brave –
Soon disappeared through the mouth of the cave.

Wi' my toor-i-a foldi-riddle-da...

There were shrieks and screams and roars and growls
Like a dying dinosaur emptying its bowels
When at last he appeared, blinking in the light
He was covered in blood – what a terrible sight.

Wi' my toor-i-a foldi-riddle-da...

Well he staggered down the hill, half pissed, half dead
Wounds on his body and wounds on his head
And he hiccupped and he giggled and he said to the chief
'Right then where's this woman wi' the two big teeth?'.

Wi' my toor-i-a foldi-riddle-da...

I heard this as a joke many years ago and fashioned it into a song, borrowing the tune from an Irish folk song. It's a great one for getting people to join in – a simple chorus, with no words to remember – and the more drams they have the more they sing it out with gusto, verve and abandon.

Snuffed Out

SONG • RECORDED ON WHISKY FOR BREAKFAST • CDTRAX361

Woke up this morning there was something wrong
My head was strangely clear
If this is being sober, I'll be glad when it's over
Bring back my whisky and beer

All day long
It's the best I'm gonna feel
What they did to me is wrong
This law should be repealed

I live in a town that's grey and damp
For the best part of the year
I don't understand why they had to ban
My whisky and my beer

All day long...

Mr Churchill likes a fat cigar
Good whisky and good jokes
But he lost his seat to a pussyfoot Pete
Who says he never drinks or smokes

Woke up this morning there was something wrong
My head was strangely clear
If this is being sober, I'll be glad when it's over
Bring back my whisky and beer

All day long...

The work of a fisherman out on the sea
Is lonely, cold and tough
When he gets ashore he likes nothing more
Than a little of the old, hard stuff

All day long...

Me and my buddies came back from the war
Soaked in blood and sweat
What could be wrong with a pint and a song
But this is all the thanks we get

Woke up this morning there was something wrong
My head was strangely clear
If this is being sober, I'll be glad when it's over
Bring back my whisky and beer

All day long...

Of course Prohibition is the antithesis of drinking to excess, though quite often, it can have the opposite effect, resulting in people going to extreme efforts to smuggle booze, make their own and drink any old crap. Scotland had its own form of Prohibition in the areas that voted for it in 1920 following the Temperance (Scotland) Act of 1913. Wick was one of those areas and resulted in the odd situation of a distillery (Old Pulteney) operating in a dry county – see also Jasper 'Jack' D.

I was invited a few years ago to be the after dinner speaker at the Old Pulteney Prohibition Ball, which incidentally celebrates the joy felt through most of the community when the 25 years of Prohibition ended. I composed this song for the occasion. A lot of good whisky was consumed at that event – I helped in a small way.

It is true, by the way, that in 1922 Edwin Scrymgeour defeated Winston Churchill, who had been MP for Dundee since 1908; Scrymgeour was the only person ever elected to the UK Parliament on a prohibitionist ticket.

Some other books published by **LUATH PRESS**

The Whisky River: Distilleries of Speyside
Robin Laing
ISBN 978-1-906817-95-4 PBK £12.99

Which river has half the distilleries in Scotland found along its length and in its surrounding glens?

Why were monks at the forefront of developing whisky?

Which Speyside distillery has an annual migration of toads?

How did Glenrothes distillery expel its ghost?

Robin Laing – singer-songwriter, author of *The Whisky Muse*, and chair of the Scotch Malt Whisky Society's Tasting Panel – set out to visit every distillery in the Speyside area, from Benromach to Tomintoul, and presents a guide to each of them here. There are descriptions of over 50 distilleries in Speyside, including The Macallan, The Glenlivet, Cardhu, Aberlour, Glenfiddich and Glengrant.

Each entry is part history, part travelogue and part commentary on the changes in the whisky industry.

Includes personal musings by the author, stories associated with the distillery and snippets of poetry and song.

Laing's 'spirit' guide in his journey is Alfred Barnard, author of 1887s *The Whisky Distilleries of the United Kingdom*. Barnard visited many of the same distilleries that Laing visits now and similarly left his impressions of the state of the facilities and the beauty of the surroundings. Much of this present book compares what Barnard found with what exists now, and the differences – and similarities – are often fascinating.

The author-singer-songwriter of The Whisky Muse *and chairperson of the Scotch Malt Whisky Society's Tasting Panel – set out to visit every distillery in the Speyside area, and presents his guide to each in this 206 page paperback. Over 50 distilleries are described, including Cardhu, Aberlour and Glen Grant. Each entry is part history, part travelogue and part commentary. Illustrated by Bob Dewar.*
THE SCOTS MAGAZINE

Robin Laing's The Whisky River *is the kind of book I immediately fall in love with, even before reading the first line. It brings together two passions of mine, whisky and song.* […] *This is essential reading for the whisky connoisseur. There might be other guide books about Scotland in general and Speyside in particular, there might be other books about Scottish whisky – but forget them, you only need this guide to the heartbeat of a small country in the North West of Europe. Slainte!* FOLKWORLD

The Whisky Muse
Scotch Whisky in Poem and Song
Robin Laing
ISBN: 9781906307448 PBK £9.99

Whisky – the water of life, perhaps Scotland's best known contribution to the world.

Muse – goddess of creative endeavour.

The Whisky Muse – the spark of inspiration to many of Scotland's great poets and songwriters.

Brought together by Robin Laing, a highly respected Scottish folk singer and songwriter, and based on his one-man show *The Angel's Share*, it combines two of his passions – folk song and whisky. Each poem and song is accompanied by fascinating additional information, and the book is full of interesting tit-bits on the process of whisky making. Reflected in these poems and songs are the pleasures (and medicinal benefits) of imbibing this most beloved of spirits as well as the unfortunate consequences of over-indulgence, the centuries of religious disapproval, the temperance movement and the exciseman. The stories told here are lubricated by warmth and companionship, best enjoyed with dram in hand. Slainte.

... necessary reading for anyone interested in whisky and song. It encapsulates Scottish folk culture and the very spirit of Scotland.
Charles McLean, Editor at Large, WHISKY MAGAZINE

Whisky Legends of Islay
Robin Laing
ISBN 978-1-906817-11-4 PBK £9.99

Why was Islay cheese banned in Italy? Why is a wall in an Islay pub covered with coins? Who is the angel that protects the distilleries? How do you prevent a wolf from coming down your chimney?

Robin Laing brings together the myths and legends of the island of Islay through its most famous export – whisky.

Ranging from the ancient legends of the seal-people to more modern tales of whisky drinkers of mythic proportions, this introduction to the whisky drinkers and producers of Islay, past and present, shows the diverse ways in which whisky forms part of island culture. With eight of the best known Scotch distilleries, it is no wonder that Islay has the reputation as the centre of whisky tourism. In weaving together the many strands of whisky-myth using stories, poems and songs, Robin Laing brings the island of Islay, and all its colourful inhabitants, to life. The witty entries are great for dipping in and out of or, alternatively, to accompany a 'wee dram'.

Some CDs by **ROBIN LAING**

The Water of Life
(Greentrax 246)

The Angels' Share
(Greentrax 137)

*Robin Laing has few superiors.
He is heard at his compelling best in*
The Angels' Share.

THE SCOTSMAN

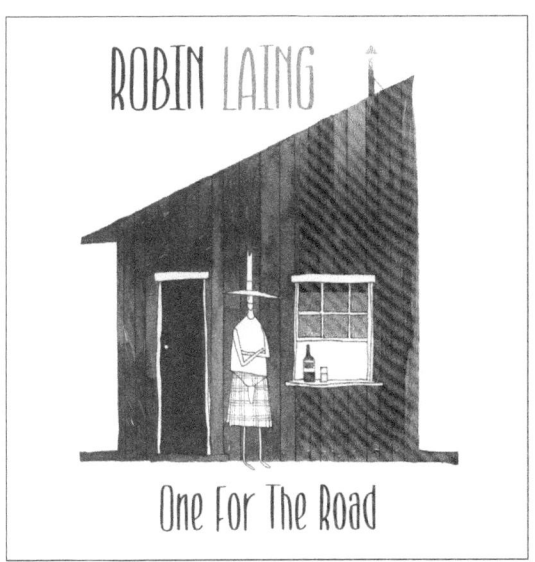

One for the Road

Yet another fantastic CD of songs for, about and sounding like good malt whisky. Even if you are a teetotaler, give this album a spin. It will intoxicate you with sounds and visions.

RAMBLES

A charming collection… this is the musical equivalent of a fine, well-aged single malt; something to be savoured during life's peaceful moments.

PENGUIN EGGS

Laing has surpassed himself with his latest recording.
One for the Road *is a glorious celebration of the 'water of life'.*

ROCK 'N' REEL

Luath Press Limited
committed to publishing well written books worth reading

LUATH PRESS takes its name from Robert Burns, whose little collie Luath (*Gael.*, swift or nimble) tripped up Jean Armour at a wedding and gave him the chance to speak to the woman who was to be his wife and the abiding love of his life. Burns called one of 'The Twa Dogs' Luath after Cuchullin's hunting dog in Ossian's *Fingal*. Luath Press was established in 1981 in the heart of Burns country, and now resides a few steps up the road from Burns' first lodgings on Edinburgh's Royal Mile.
Luath offers you distinctive writing with a hint of unexpected pleasures.

Most bookshops in the UK, the US, Canada, Australia, New Zealand and parts of Europe either carry our books in stock or can order them for you. To order direct from us, please send a £sterling cheque, postal order, international money order or your credit card details (number, address of cardholder and expiry date) to us at the address below. Please add post and packing as follows: UK – £1.00 per delivery address; overseas surface mail – £2.50 per delivery address; overseas airmail – £3.50 for the first book to each delivery address, plus £1.00 for each additional book by airmail to the same address. If your order is a gift, we will happily enclose your card or message at no extra charge.

Luath Press Limited
543/2 Castlehill
The Royal Mile
Edinburgh EH1 2ND
Scotland
Telephone: 0131 225 4326 (24 hours)
email: sales@luath.co.uk
Website: www.luath.co.uk